Wee Can™ Count

Teaching Beginning Mathematics
Using Renowned Children's
Literature for Grades K & 1

by Carolyn McMahon and Peggy Warrick

Portland, Oregon

2007

NWREL
Northwest Regional Educational Laboratory

Northwest Regional Educational Laboratory
101 S.W. Main Street, Suite 500
Portland, Oregon 97204
Telephone: 503-275-9500
E-mail: info@nwrel.org
Web site: www.nwrel.org

Carolyn McMahon and Peggy Warrick, Authors

To order, telephone 888-827-7241
Learn more about the 6+1 Trait® Writing Model at www.TheTraits.org

ISBN 978-089354-107-1

Contents

The Learning Centers

Preface

This book was written by and for teachers who seek creative ways to introduce basic mathematical concepts to kindergarten and first-grade students while sharing classic children's literature. Using favorite stories helps students strengthen their reading skills as it sets the stage for learning mathematics. Additionally, *Wee Can Count*™ continues the work of *Wee Can Write*™ by integrating writing across the activities and learning centers.

While *Wee Can Count* is primarily designed for teachers at the K–1 level, many second-grade teachers will find the activities appropriate as well. Each learning center has a section titled "Math Focus" to link the activities to mathematics in a variety of important areas:
• Numbers and Operations
• Algebra
• Geometry
• Measurement
• Data Analysis and Probability
• Problem Solving
• Representation

• Reasoning and Proof
• Communication
· Connections

We don't intend for *Wee Can Count* to be an introduction to the 6+1 Trait® Writing Model of Instruction & Assessment created by the Northwest Regional Educational Laboratory (NWREL). However, we have included information on the original six traits starting on page xiv, along with a description of how the traits play out for early writers. We hope teachers using this book have had some instruction in the model before using it to guide and assess student writing. For information about 6+1 Trait® Writing and training opportunities, visit www.TheTraits.org/ or call NWREL at 1-800-547-6339.

Enjoy opening a new world of learning to your young students!

About the Authors

Peggy and Carolyn are the authors of the popular *Wee Can Write*™. They continue to work together creating easy-to-use materials for teaching the 6+1 Trait® Writing Model of Instruction & Assessment across the curriculum.

Peggy Warrick, from Cheyenne, Wyoming, received a degree in special education and elementary education from the University of Wyoming. She has worked in resource and general education classrooms for 17 years. Peggy has also worked as a consultant to integrate special needs students into general education classrooms. Experienced with all grade levels, Peggy understands the need for a firm beginning foundation for all students. Her joy has been to create and provide support for early elementary teachers to simplify their task of building a strong foundation in the writing process.

Carolyn McMahon is a high-energy and literature-loving kindergarten teacher. Having spent 16 years in education, including kindergarten, first, and second grades, and four years as an elementary librarian, her current passion is writing with the youngest students. Carolyn is a graduate of Quincy University in Quincy, Illinois, with degrees in English and library science. She also has an endorsement in elementary education from the University of Colorado, Colorado Springs. Carolyn has taught across the United States, from California to Washington, D.C. Her wealth of experience, positive outlook, and wit are evidenced in her writing contributions and workshop presentations.

Dedication

With thanks to students and teachers past, present, and future who continue to be our inspiration.

How To Use This Book

Introduction to *Wee Can Count*™

If you are a teacher of the very young child you have been waiting and wanting and dreaming of this book! We have created an answer to what we know is every teacher's dream: Learning centers that are ready to use! Out-of-the-book ready! Life is simple and sweet ready! "I can't believe you did this for me" ready!

This book introduces numbers and basic mathematics to kindergarten and first-grade students through popular children's literature. While not the primary focus, *Wee Can Count* continues the work of *Wee Can Write*™ by incorporating writing across the curriculum using the 6+1 Trait® Writing Model of Instruction & Assessment.

The titles included in *Wee Can Count* are classics and are widely available through local libraries, classroom collections, or book club offerings. We have created six activities for each piece of literature. The student instructions are ready to display. The necessary materials are listed for ease of gathering. All reproducible items—student worksheets and resource pages—are ready to copy and use. A Math Focus Area is highlighted in the teacher overview. Student evaluations, called "check-ups" in this book, and student worksheets for teachers to assess student understanding are provided for each activity. The books we chose enhance thematic connections to units that may be used throughout the school year.

"How do I begin?"

Assembling the Materials

Assembling learning centers can be overwhelming ... gathering the books, pencils, crayons, paper, and completing general preparations can be a daunting task. In each activity's teacher instructions is a list of all the essential materials students will need for that activity. The list is basic: You can streamline or enhance it. The most important item for the learning center is the "introduction" page.

Carefully read this page for each activity before you place students in the centers to ensure you have included all the necessary materials and that the rebus-like directions are clear to you. Learning centers look different everywhere. Some classrooms have specific areas, some use desks, and some have designated tables for center activities. The *Wee Can Count* centers are portable. They will fit anywhere you have space.

Setting Up

To set up the learning centers, photocopy the student activities and any worksheets or resource pages called for at each center. The student activity instructions can be laminated so that you can use them repeatedly. A set of laminated, color instructions is available from the Northwest Regional Educational Laboratory; to order, call 1-888-827-7241).

The reproducibles (student worksheets, resource pages, check-up packets) should be duplicated for each student. Several pages in this book should be copied in color: pp. 38, 41, 43, 44, 51, 52, 53, 83, 85, and 141. Attach the student instructions to a sturdy display that's clearly visible in the learning center. Place all materials for the learning center at the work table. Use whatever method works best for you. *Wee Can Count* learning centers are ready to use!

Working With Learning Centers

Learning centers, when done properly and purposefully, facilitate independent learning and help children take responsibility for completing their work. The centers also assist the teacher in her ability to multitask and accomplish small-group writing, reading, mathematical problem solving, or individual assessment. Center work that can be done independently by the student is an important part of any early childhood classroom routine and needs to have a purpose, a teacher assessment component—in this case the Student Worksheet—and self-evaluation by the student, the check-up.

It is always a goal to give students a choice in center work. Experience tells us that sometimes choices can be overwhelming, too. Learning centers create an opportunity to increase peer relationships in a positive manner. It is a chance for those students who may need a partner to have the "right" partner for a center job. All students will get to all six centers per literature title. Avoid the "I want to be with …" and "I don't like that center because…" complaints.

Assigning your students to centers may be the best choice in your classroom. Students will be on task and working quickly and purposefully if they "see and go" right to their assigned center. Activities in these centers are designed to be accomplished in 20 to 30 minutes. (However, recognize that students have varied working rates.) Efficient use of time in any classroom is essential. Teachers can help improve efficiency by taking away some of the "guesswork" and placing the students into centers.

A Little Help, Please

Some of the activities in the learning centers may require a helper for work completion. If you don't have an educational aide in your classroom, it is a good idea to invite parents or students from the upper grades to help monitor the centers. Parents can be very helpful. Because the directions and materials are at the center, the parents can clearly see what is expected of the students without lengthy teacher instruction. It is wise, however, to have an initial training to explain the learning centers and the parent's role as helper at the beginning of the school year.

"Where Do I Go?"

Who hasn't heard that? Each teacher finds a method that works the best for her. There are creative tools and products that can indicate where a student is to work. A simple display of the unit activities and students' names on a chart or on a poster, makes getting there quick and easy. It is important to record when a student has been to a center to avoid duplicating or missing a learning center. Using a simple teacher-created spreadsheet or table may assist you in this task. Record the date the child worked in that center. Use the check-ups cover sheet with the six activities to record dates and any anecdotal information for your assessment and for parent information. Another simple solution is to use a copy of your daily attendance sheet with the six activities listed across the top with an entry indicating when the activity was completed.

Example:

One Hundred Hungry Ants

	Learning Center 1	Learning Center 2	Learning Center 3	Learning Center 4	Learning Center 5	Learning Center 6
Anne	Feb 16	Feb 17				
Tiffany		Feb 16	Feb 17			
Rob			Feb 16		Feb 17	
Peggy			Feb 16			Feb 17

Before you begin, explain all of the centers to students in a whole group. They may not remember all of the details, but it will give them an idea of what is to be done at each center. If you choose to finish one center in a day, it takes six days to finish the rotation of one book.

"File, Please!"

You will see at the bottom of each learning center direction sheet the request to "File your work, please." Keeping accurate and thorough records is vital in any classroom, but in the pre-kindergarten, kindergarten, and primary grades, record keeping is essential. A simple hanging file folder system where students can place their work after each center session is a workable solution. Arrange the hanging folders alphabetically by first name. When the student is finished with the activity, there is a student "check-up" for each center. This needs to be filled out completely by the student and filed with his or her completed center work. Enrichment activities should be provided for students who finish center work ahead of others.

It is helpful in the management of center time to have a specific routine of where and how student work is to be filed or stored and what students are to do when they have completed a center.

Each *Wee Can Count* unit has a check-up cover sheet with space provided for the teacher's anecdotal notes. Copy the cover sheet and label it with the student's name. Gluing this sheet to a folded 12 x 18-inch sheet of construction paper serves two purposes: the teacher can record the date and notes on this sheet when the child was in that center and parents can easily check their child's work. Placing all work in the "folder" and sending it home with the child is a wonderful opportunity for parents to be included and observe the progress of their student.

Math Focus

The *Wee Can Count* learning centers are created to introduce the use of numbers and basic mathematics. The Math Focus is stated in the introduction to each learning center activity. The focus may be applied to the objectives and benchmarks specified by an individual district.

The activities link to mathematics in numerous areas:

1. Number and Operations
2. Algebra
3. Geometry
4. Measurement
5. Data Analysis and Probability
6. Problem Solving
7. Reasoning and Proof
8. Communication
9. Connections
10. Representation

Writing Across the Curriculum

Selected activities include a student writing component that can be assessed using the 6+1 Trait® Writing Model. This book is not intended to be an instruction or usage manual for the model. However, we have included the following primer on the definitions of each trait and how they look at the K–1 level. We've also included the 6+1 Trait® Writing Assessment for Beginning Writers Rubric (page 177) to guide the assessment of student writing. Instructions on implementing the 6+1 Trait® Writing Model for young writers can be found in the guidebook *Seeing With New Eyes*.

Trait Definitions

IDEAS are the heart of the message, the content of the piece, and the main theme, together with all the details that enrich and develop that theme. When the ideas are strong, the message is clear, and the storyline is easy to follow. Things make sense. The secret lies in the details: strong writing always includes details that are clear, accurate, and less than obvious.

Successful writers do not spend time telling readers what they already know: Penguins are black and white, penguins live in Antarctica, penguins love to eat fish. They seek out details a reader might not know: Penguins swim well because they are shaped like torpedoes. Penguins are territorial and like some space around themselves and their nests. They will launch themselves at anyone who comes too close.

How This Looks at the Primary Level

At the primary level, we need to look for details in children's artwork and listen for important details in the stories they tell verbally long before they begin to create extended written text. Encourage students first to be gatherers and collectors of information, as well as observers of life; to look carefully at the world around them; and to share orally what they see through their pictures and through their text. Later, as they write more, look for focus, meaning, a clear message or story, strong details, and direct statements such as "I like horses." When you see these things, help children see the power of their own writing, too!

Look also for complexity, such as lots of lines and lots of color in pictures, along with important little details that would have been easy to gloss over—veins in leaves, birds or insects with wings and legs, expressions on faces, details like buttons or shoelaces, signs of movement (a person running or waving, a bird poised for flight), words woven into pictures, perspective (small to large), or pictures that extend off the page.

• •

ORGANIZATION is the internal structure of writing, like the framework of a building or the skeleton of an animal. It holds things together and gives the whole piece form and shape. Good organization helps a reader understand a writer's message and follow a story with ease. A writer with strong organization stays focused on one key idea (in informational writing) or one main plot (in a story). The writer also fills the text (and sometimes the pictures) with little clues that tie the ideas together, and build transitions from one idea or event to the next. When the organization is strong, the beginning builds a sense of anticipation in the reader and the ending wraps things up in a satisfying way.

How This Looks at the Primary Level

At the primary level, think balance and harmony. Early signs of organization include filling the page with text or pictures in a balanced way; literally organizing text, art, and white space; and creating labels, titles, or other text that harmonize with a picture. Gradually, primary writers also develop a sense of sequencing that may begin with chronological storytelling, followed by grouping similar bits together in informational writing. This kind of beginning structure may show up in picture sequences first, then in multiple-sentence text. Primary writers may also develop a strong sense of beginning and ending from listening to text long before they are able to reproduce these features in their own writing.

• •

VOICE is the writer coming through the writing. It is the heart and soul of the writing—the magic, the wit, the feeling, the risk taking. It is unique to each writer. When a writer is engaged personally with the topic and aware of communicating with an audience through the choice of content and expressive language, a very personal flavor emanates from the writing. It is that individual something—different from the mark of all other writers—that we call voice.

How This Looks at the Primary Level

Individuality! Sparkle! Love of writing and drawing, of life itself! Exuberance! Humor! Playfulness! Emotion on the faces of the characters! The extraordinary! These are the signs of voice. At the primary level, voice is first noticeable in speaking, oral storytelling, and art. It is individual expression, independence, liveliness. In art, it may show up as a kind of energy in the work. It may reveal itself through facial expressions or pictures that create tension or a sense of anticipation in the viewer through the unusual use of details. Writers/artists with strong voice find their own paths through pictures, and later through words and ideas in text. Their work tends to look or sound different from others. It gets our attention. And it often makes us say, "Oh, I know whose picture writing that is." The something that tells you is voice.

● ●

WORD CHOICE is the use of rich, colorful, precise language that communicates not just in a functional way, but in a way that moves and enlightens the reader. In good descriptive writing, strong word choice paints pictures in the reader's mind. In informational writing, strong word choice clarifies, explains, and expands ideas. In persuasive writing, strong word choice compels the reader to see things more clearly and, sometimes, to validate a writer's position. Effective word choice is characterized not so much by exceptional vocabulary as by the ability to use everyday language naturally and in a fresh or unexpected way.

How This Looks at the Primary Level

Primary writers/artists may express strong word choice in their oral storytelling or other sharing long before they write many words at all. Early on, we can listen for original expression and note students' curiosity about word meanings or usage. As children begin to write words, look first for the understanding that letters form words and that written words communicate a specific meaning. Later, look both for correct word use and for originality, including a willingness to experiment—to try new words recently heard, or even to invent words. Look also for images, pictures, and ideas that evoke particular words or phrases: "When I look at this picture, the word that comes into my mind is _____."

In text, look for verbs, lots of active verbs—words that show action, energy, and movement. Verbs are important because they give the reader more information per word than any other part of speech.

Unusual, precise, or well-used nouns, adjectives, and adverbs are important, too. Look for the unexpected, the writer who is stretching.

• •

SENTENCE FLUENCY is the rhythm and flow of the language, the sound of word patterns, the way in which the writing plays to the ear, not just the eye. How does it sound when read aloud? That's the test. Fluent writing has cadence, power, rhythm, and movement. It is free of awkward patterns that slow down a reader and cause the reader to stumble or reread. Sentences vary in both length and style, and are so well-crafted that reading aloud is a pleasure.

How This Looks at the Primary Level

Most children do not write complete sentences at the beginning of their primary years. We cannot look at sentence length or patterns at first. We will find these things as soon as they develop. Until then, listen for rhythm and cadence in oral language and notice how the writer attends, as a listener, to rhythm in the language you share orally. Is the listener in tune with your sentence patterns, rhythmic language (such as poetry), or rhymes? Can your listeners/writers tell a sentence from a fragment or phrase? Can they tell rhythmic language from language that is choppy?

They will write what they hear. They will learn fluency as listeners first, then gradually reflect what they hear in the beat of their own text.

Once the sentences begin to flow, look beyond punctuation. Listen for the rhythm. Listen to this second-grader's words about poetry:

What Is Poetry?
poetry is moosick to me
On a pees of paper
moosick that rimes,
soft moosick to my ers

Always look at sentence beginnings. When you see differences, let the writer know you noticed. Does one sentence begin in a way that hooks it to the preceding sentence? The following are some examples: at the same time; then; next; but; when that happened; later; the next day.

These links are important. They show logic and connection. Are some sentences longer? You can point this out. But mostly, hear the sound. Hear the beat. Read aloud. Enjoy the flow.

• •

CONVENTIONS are textual traditions. They have grown out of the need for conformity to make text easier to follow. Anything a professional proofreader deals with in getting text ready for publication falls under this heading: spelling, punctuation, grammar and usage, paragraphing, and capitalization. Neatness, while important, is not considered part of conventions. It is included in the 6+1 Trait® Writing Model in the trait of "presentation."

How This Looks at the Primary Level

Primary students are natural borrowers, and their knowledge of conventions shows up first in their borrowing. Keep in mind that even the simplest things—such as writing from left to right, beginning at the top of the page and working downward, facing Es the same way all the time, putting spaces between words—must ALL be learned. No writer is born knowing these things. All are conventions of our accepted writing style. Notice and acknowledge these beginning conventions to give your primary writers a legitimate sense of their true accomplishment.

Discovery of periods or quotation marks (or any mark of punctuation) is cause for celebration—regardless of whether those marks are correctly placed. Exploration is a vital steppingstone on the path to correctness. The writer who discovers periods will also soon discover how and when to use them.

Similarly, students must first associate sounds (consonant sounds, then vowels) with letters and play with letter strings to form words before moving to prephonetic, phonetic, and close-to-correct or correct spelling. Readable spelling is a fine goal at the primary level.

Conventionally correct spelling is a lifelong goal that virtually no one (including professional editors) masters totally without the support of helpful resources such as dictionaries and spell checkers.

Next look for creative and persistent borrowing. Reward your students for noticing the print around them—provide plenty of it—and for being curious enough to ask questions. Encourage guessing about what a group of letters might spell or what a mark of punctuation might mean. This is a time of exploration, and the exploration itself is a major goal for the primary years—and for as long as we want writers to keep learning. If you doubt its importance, visit a high school or freshman English classroom and ask how many students have recently read a style handbook or dictionary for fun, added a new convention to their editing repertoire, or showed enough curiosity about a mark of punctuation to ask how or why it was invented.

Applying the writing rubric to center work has purpose, whether done by the student or by the teacher. Use of the rubric is also helpful to the parent to understand the performance level of his or her child's writing. It gives parents a vision of realistic writing expectations for the early education years.

Note: While the 6+1 Trait® Writing Model includes the trait of presentation, kindergarten is a little early in the process of writing development to include it in this book. There may be times, however, when you decide that a conversation about presentation with a wee writer is entirely appropriate.

Applying the 6+1 Trait® Writing Assessment for Beginning Writers Rubric to center work is useful in assessing student writing. It can also be a helpful tool for parents to understand the level of writing their child is currently demonstrating. And, it gives parents a vision of what good writing expectations are for the early education years.

Get Ready! Get Set! Go!

Learning centers ready to go! Teachers ready to teach! Students ready to learn! *Wee Can Count* makes it easy for you to integrate the writing process with the mathematics curriculum. We hope you enjoy these activities in your classroom centers as much as we enjoyed creating them for you!

Example of Scoring Student Writing

Students	Learning Center 1	Learning Center 2	Learning Center 3	Learning Center 4	Learning Center 5	Learning Center 6
Adams, K.	3	1	5	2	6	4
Case, J.	1	2	6	3	5	4
Hall, B.	3	4	1	2	6	5
Miller, E.	2	1	3	6	4	5
Smith, N.	4	6	2	5	1	3
Wall, C.	5	3	4	1	2	6
This chart is for teacher use.						

6+1 Trait® Writing Assessment for Beginning Writers

1) EXPERIMENTING	2) EMERGING	3) DEVELOPING	4) CAPABLE	5) EXPERIENCED
Ideas	**Ideas**	**Ideas**	**Ideas**	**Ideas**
❏ Uses scribbles for writing	❏ Some recognizable words present	❏ Attempts a story or to make a point	❏ Writing tells a story or makes a point	❏ Presents a fresh/ original idea
❏ Dictates labels or a story	❏ Labels pictures	❏ Illustration supports the writing	❏ Illustration (if present) enhances writing	❏ Topic is narrowed and focused
❏ Shapes that look like letters	❏ Uses drawings that show detail	❏ Meaning of the general idea is recognizable	❏ Idea is generally on topic	❏ Develops one clear, main idea
❏ Line forms that imitate text	❏ Pictures supported by some words	❏ Some ideas clear but some are still fuzzy	❏ Details are present but not developed	❏ Uses interesting, important details for support
❏ Writes letters randomly				❏ Writer understands topic well
Organization	**Organization**	**Organization**	**Organization**	**Organization**
❏ Ability to order or group not yet present	❏ No title (if requested)	❏ A title is present (if requested)	❏ An appropriate title is present (if requested)	❏ An original title is present (if requested)
❏ No sense of beginning or end	❏ Experiments with beginnings	❏ Limited transitions present	❏ Attempts transitions from sentence to sentence	❏ Transitions connect main ideas
❏ Connections between ideas are confusing	❏ Begins to group similar words/pictures	❏ Beginning but no ending except "The End"	❏ Beginning works well and attempts an ending	❏ The opening attracts
	❏ Transitions or evidence of sequencing haphazard	❏ Attempts at sequencing and transitions	❏ Logical sequencing	❏ An effective ending is tried
			❏ Key ideas begin to surface	❏ Easy to follow
				❏ Important ideas stand out
Voice	**Voice**	**Voice**	**Voice**	**Voice**
❏ Communicates feeling with size, color, shape, line in drawing, or letter imitation	❏ Hints of voice present in words and phrases	❏ Expresses some predictable feelings	❏ Writing is individual and expressive	❏ Uses text to elicit a variety of emotion
❏ Work is similar to everyone else's	❏ Looks different from most others	❏ Moments of individual sparkle, but then hides	❏ Individual perspective becomes evident	❏ Takes some risks to say more than what is expected
❏ Unclear response to task	❏ Energy/mood is present	❏ Repetition of familiar ideas reduces energy	❏ Personal treatment of a standard topic	❏ Point of view is evident
❏ No awareness of audience	❏ Treatment of topic predictable	❏ Awareness that the writing will be read by someone else	❏ Writes to convey a story or idea to the reader	❏ Writes with a clear sense of audience
	❏ Audience is fuzzy—could be anybody, anywhere	❏ Reader has limited connection to writer	❏ Attempts non-standard point of view	❏ Cares deeply about the topic

Word Choice	Word Choice	Word Choice	Word Choice	Word Choice
❏ Writes letters in strings	❏ Recognizable words	❏ General or ordinary words	❏ Uses favorite words correctly	❏ Everyday words used well
❏ Imitates word patterns	❏ Environmental words used correctly	❏ Attempts new words but they don't always fit	❏ Experiments with new and different words with some success	❏ Precise, accurate, fresh, original words
❏ Pictures stand for words and phrases	❏ Attempts at phrases	❏ Settles for the word or phrase that "will do"	❏ Tries to choose words for specificity	❏ Creates vivid images in a natural way
❏ Copies environmental print	❏ Functional language	❏ Big words used only to impress reader	❏ Attempts to use descriptive words to create images	❏ Avoids repetition, clichés, or vague language
		❏ Relies on slang, clichés, or repetition		❏ Attempts at figurative language

Sentence Fluency	Sentence Fluency	Sentence Fluency	Sentence Fluency	Sentence Fluency
❏ Mimics letters and words across the page	❏ Strings words together into phrases	❏ Uses simple sentences	❏ Simple and compound sentences present and effective	❏ Consistently uses sentence variety
❏ Words stand alone	❏ Attempts simple sentences	❏ Sentences tend to begin the same	❏ Attempts complex sentences	❏ Sentence structure is correct and creative
❏ Patterns for sentences not in evidence	❏ Short, repetitive sentence patterns	❏ Experiments with other sentence patterns	❏ Not all sentences begin the same	❏ Variety of sentence beginnings
❏ Sentence sense not yet present	❏ Dialogue present but not understandable	❏ Reader may have to reread to follow meaning	❏ Sections of writing have rhythm and flow	❏ Natural rhythm, cadence, and flow
		❏ Dialogue present but needs interpretation		❏ Sentences have texture that clarify the important idea

Conventions	Conventions	Conventions	Conventions	Conventions
❏ Writes letter strings (pre-phonetic: dmRxzz)	❏ Attempts semi-phonetic spelling (MTR, UM, KD, etc.)	❏ Uses phonetic spelling (MOTR, HUMN, KLOSD, etc.) on personal words	❏ Transitional spelling on less frequent words (MONSTUR, HUMUN, CLOSSED, etc.)	❏ Frequently used words are spelled correctly and very close on other words
❏ Attempts to create standard letters	❏ Uses mixed upper- and lower-case letters	❏ Spelling of frequently used words still spotty	❏ Spelling of frequently used words usually correct	❏ Capitals used for obvious proper nouns as well as sentences
❏ Attempts spacing of words, letters, symbols, or pictures	❏ Uses spaces between letters and words	❏ Uses capitals at the beginning of sentences	❏ Capitals at the beginning of sentences and variable use of proper nouns	❏ Basic punctuation is used correctly and/or creatively
❏ Attempts to write left to right	❏ Consistently writes left to right	❏ Usually uses ending punctuation		❏ Indents consistently to show paragraphs
				❏ Shows control over standard grammar

One Hundred Hungry Ants

by Elinor J. Pinczes (Author) & Bonnie MacKain (Illustrator)

Who doesn't love a PICNIC?

These ants sure do, and if they ever get there they will enjoy a feast! But, they cannot decide HOW to get there. Should they march in 10 rows of 10? Or by four rows of 25? Better yet, in two rows of 50? One brave ant suggests a variety of ways to travel. So, "a hey and a hi dee ho," it's off to count we go!

Learning Center 1
Introduction

Directions

Students will read and retell the story *One Hundred Hungry Ants* in a group setting. After reading, individual students will draw a detailed picture and include specific items seen in the story. Following the directions will enable the student to create a clear picture that demonstrates understanding of the story.

Materials

- *One Hundred Hungry Ants* (one per student)
- Crayons
- Pencils
- Drawing paper

Math Focus

Number and Operations
Understand numbers, ways of representing numbers, relationships among numbers, and number systems
- Count with understanding and recognize "how many" in sets of objects

Communication
Communicate mathematical thinking coherently and clearly to peers, teachers, and others

Learning Center 1

You will need these materials:
- Pencils
- Crayons
- *One Hundred Hungry Ants*
- Paper

1. Read and retell *One Hundred Hungry Ants* with your friends.

2. Draw a detailed picture to tell about what you see in *One Hundred Hungry Ants*. Use crayons and paper.

3. Draw your favorite animals from the story.

4. Add three (3) trees.

5. Add six (6) ants.

6. Add one (1) picnic basket.

7. Write a YUMMY sentence to describe your picture.

8. File your work and quick check, please.

Learning Center 2
Introduction

Directions

This activity focuses on the students' ability to show sequential events in *One Hundred Hungry Ants*. Students will draw a numerical representation of the ants' movements at the beginning of the story and at the end.

Materials

- Crayons
- Pencils
- *One Hundred Hungry Ants* (one per student)
- Drawing paper

Math Focus

Number and Operations

Understand numbers, ways of representing numbers, relationships among numbers, and number systems

- Count with understanding and recognize "how many" in sets of objects

- Use multiple models to develop initial understandings of place value and the base-10 number system

Understand meanings of operations and how they relate to one another
- Understand various meanings of addition and subtraction of whole numbers and the relationship between the two operations
- Understand the effects of adding and subtracting whole numbers

Representation
Create and use representations to organize, record, and communicate mathematical ideas

Reasoning
Make and investigate mathematical conjectures

Learning Center 2

You will need these materials:
- Pencils
- Crayons
- *One Hundred Hungry Ants*
- Paper

Book

CRAYON

1. Fold your paper in half .
   - Label one side beginning.
   - Label one side ending.

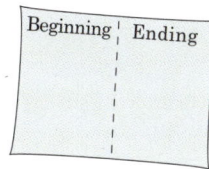

   Beginning | Ending

2. Draw a picture of the beginning of the story.

   - How many ants did you draw?
   - Have a friend count and check your work.

3. Draw a picture of the ants at the end of the story.
   - Draw 10 lines of 10 ants.
   - Label your sets of ants.

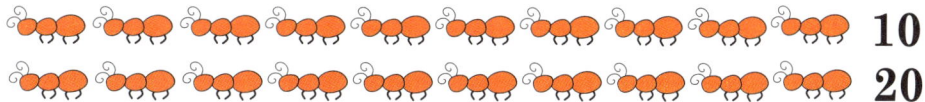

   10
   20

   - Have a friend count and check your work.

4. File your work and quick check, please.

   Quick Check

Learning Center 3
Introduction

Directions

This activity emphasizes individual expression, as students imagine they are very hungry ants on the way to finding delicious treats to eat. Using descriptive words about foods and number words to tell how many goodies they could eat, each student will write a sentence on a paper plate.

Materials

- Student worksheet: Paper plate (one per student)
- Resource page: Number words (one per student)
- Crayons
- Pencils
- Optional: magazines with food pictures for nonwriters to cut and glue to their plates

Math Focus

Number and Operations

Understand numbers, ways of representing numbers, relationships among numbers, and number systems

- Count with understanding and recognize "how many" in sets of objects
- Develop understanding of the relative position and magnitude of whole numbers and of ordinal and cardinal numbers and their connections

Learning Center 3

You will need these materials:
- Pencils
- Crayons CRAYON
- Paper plate
- Number words Words!

You will be writing a page of our class book, *These Ants Love to Eat.*

1.   You are a very hungry ant!

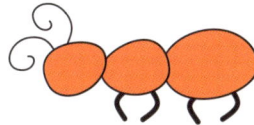

2.   In your best ant "voice" describe how hungry you are!
     Write what your favorite ant treat is to eat.
     Be sure to include number words and delicious words
     in your writing. Draw a picture to match
     your favorite foods.

3.   Here is an example:
     I am one starving ant!
     I could eat two (2) crispy carrots,
     three (3) sweet apples,
     and one (1) hot pancake!
     Yummy in my tummy!

4.   Write your own ideas on your plate.
     Bring your plate to the teacher for our class book.

Number Words

1 one	11 eleven
2 two	12 twelve
3 three	13 thirteen
4 four	14 fourteen
5 five	15 fifteen
6 six	16 sixteen
7 seven	17 seventeen
8 eight	18 eighteen
9 nine	19 nineteen
10 ten	20 twenty

Paper Plate

I am one _____ ant!

I could eat _____,

_____,

and _____.

Name _____

Learning Center 4
Introduction

Directions

The juicy, interesting, and lively words that appear in *One Hundred Hungry Ants* provide an activity that students will successfully complete independently. Sorting the words on the "word sorting page" by number of letters will reinforce students' understanding that letters make up words, develop recognition of some high-frequency words, and develop initial decoding skills.

One-to-one counting and sorting into groups is an additional math skills focus. Writing a sentence using one or two of the sorted words may be just the right challenge for these early writers.

Materials

- Crayons
- Pencils
- Scissors
- Glue
- Resource page: Word sorting (one per student)
- Drawing paper

Math Focus

Number and Operations
Understand numbers, ways of representing numbers, relationships among numbers, and number systems
- Count with understanding and recognize "how many" in sets of objects
- Develop understanding of the relative position and magnitude of whole numbers and of ordinal and cardinal numbers and their connections

Data Analysis and Probability
Formulate questions that can be addressed with data and collect, organize, and display relevant data to answer them
- Sort and classify objects according to their attributes and organize data about the objects
- Represent data using concrete objects, pictures, and graph

Algebra
Understand patterns, relations, and functions
- Sort, classify, and order objects by size, number, and other properties

Learning Center 4

You will need these materials:
- Crayons
- Pencils
- Scissors
- Glue
- Word sorting page
- Drawing paper

1. Fold your drawing paper in fourths. Number each square like this:

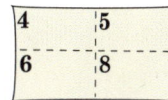

2. Cut out the interesting words on your word sorting page. Sort the words by the number of letters in them. You can read these words in the book *One Hundred Hungry Ants*.

3. Glue your words into the numbered squares on your drawing paper.

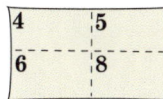

4. On the back of the page use at least one word in a terrific sentence. Use your best handwriting! Draw a picture to match your words.

5. File your work and quick check, please.

Word Sorting

lines	food	sunshine
hill	forest	field
picnic	cross	marching
hungry	ants	breeze
littlest	down	swarming
that	rumbling	soft

Learning Center 5
Introduction

Directions

Students will assemble strips into the verses of the familiar song "The Ants Go Marching." Then they will read and sing the song together as a cooperative group.

Students will demonstrate their understanding of the math term "array" as they use drawing and writing to represent groups of ants in arrays.

Materials

- Resource page: Chart of the song "The Ants Go Marching" (one per student, plus one enlarged copy for classroom wall)
- Verse strips of the song "The Ants Go Marching" placed in clear bags/envelopes (one set per student)
- Resource page: Number words
- Construction paper (12 x 18)
- Glue
- Crayons
- Pencils

Math Focus

Number and Operations
Understand numbers, ways of representing numbers, relationships among numbers, and number systems
- Count with understanding and recognize "how many" in sets of objects
- Connect number words and numerals to the quantities they represent, using various physical models and representations

Understand meanings of operations and how they relate to one another
- Understand situations that entail multiplication and division, such as equal groupings of objects and sharing equally

Problem Solving
Apply and adapt a variety of appropriate strategies to solve problems

Communication
Communicate mathematical thinking coherently and clearly to peers, teachers, and others

Learning Center 5

You will need these materials:
- Pencils
- Crayons
- Glue
- Number words
- A copy of the song "The Ants Go Marching"
- Verse strips in a bag
- Construction paper

1. Read the song from the class chart with your friends. Use the song sheets to help you.

2. Put the verse strips in your baggie in the correct number order. Work together with your friends. Read or sing the song.

   The ants marched one by one,
   and two by two,
   three by three,
   and even ten by ten!

3. Glue the verses on your paper.

4. Sing the song with your friends!

5. File your work and quick check, please.

The Ants Go Marching

The ants go marching one by one, hurrah, hurrah
The ants go marching one by one, hurrah, hurrah
The ants go marching one by one,
The little one stops to suck his thumb
And they all go marching down to the ground
To get out of the rain, BOOM! BOOM! BOOM!

The ants go marching two by two, hurrah, hurrah
The ants go marching two by two, hurrah, hurrah
The ants go marching two by two,
The little one stops to tie his shoe
And they all go marching down to the ground
To get out of the rain, BOOM! BOOM! BOOM!

The ants go marching three by three, hurrah, hurrah
The ants go marching three by three, hurrah, hurrah
The ants go marching three by three,
The little one stops to climb a tree
And they all go marching down to the ground
To get out of the rain, BOOM! BOOM! BOOM!

The ants go marching four by four, hurrah, hurrah
The ants go marching four by four, hurrah, hurrah
The ants go marching four by four,
The little one stops to shut the door
And they all go marching down to the ground
To get out of the rain, BOOM! BOOM! BOOM!

The ants go marching five by five, hurrah, hurrah
The ants go marching five by five, hurrah, hurrah
The ants go marching five by five,
The little one stops to take a dive
And they all go marching down to the ground
To get out of the rain, BOOM! BOOM! BOOM!

The ants go marching six by six, hurrah, hurrah
The ants go marching six by six, hurrah, hurrah
The ants go marching six by six,
The little one stops to pick up sticks
And they all go marching down to the ground
To get out of the rain, BOOM! BOOM! BOOM!

The ants go marching seven by seven, hurrah, hurrah
The ants go marching seven by seven, hurrah, hurrah
The ants go marching seven by seven,
The little one stops to pray to heaven
And they all go marching down to the ground
To get out of the rain, BOOM! BOOM! BOOM!

The ants go marching eight by eight, hurrah, hurrah
The ants go marching eight by eight, hurrah, hurrah
The ants go marching eight by eight,
The little one stops to shut the gate
And they all go marching down to the ground
To get out of the rain, BOOM! BOOM! BOOM!

The ants go marching nine by nine, hurrah, hurrah
The ants go marching nine by nine, hurrah, hurrah
The ants go marching nine by nine,
The little one stops to check the time
And they all go marching down to the ground
To get out of the rain, BOOM! BOOM! BOOM!

The ants go marching ten by ten, hurrah, hurrah
The ants go marching ten by ten, hurrah, hurrah
The ants go marching ten by ten,
The little one stops to say "THE END"
And they all go marching down to the ground
To get out of the rain, BOOM! BOOM! BOOM!

Learning Center 6
Introduction

Directions

The recognition of basic punctuation marks (period, comma, exclamation mark, and question mark) is emphasized in this activity using the song "The Ants Go Marching." Students will draw a designated shape with a specific color to show their knowledge of punctuation marks. Additionally, the students will identify the title of the song.

Materials

- Resource page: "The Ants Go Marching" from previous lesson (one per student)
- Crayons
- Pencils

Math Focus

Number and Operations

Understand numbers, ways of representing numbers, relationships among numbers, and number systems

- Count with understanding and recognize "how many" in sets of objects

Geometry

Analyze characteristics and properties of two-and three-dimensional geometric shapes and develop mathematical arguments about geometric relationships

- Recognize, name, build, draw, compare, and sort two- and three-dimensional shapes

Learning Center 6

You will need these materials:
- A copy of the song "The Ants Go Marching"
- Crayons
- Pencils

1. Look for the punctuation marks in "The Ants Go Marching."

2. Draw a red square around each period (•).

3. Draw a yellow circle around each comma (,).

4. Draw an orange triangle around each exclamation mark. (!)

5. Draw a blue rectangle around the title of the song.

6. Can you sing the song with your friends? Sing the song in an inside voice, please!

7. File your work and quick check, please.

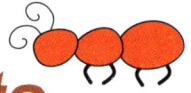

One Hundred Hungry Ants

Learning Center 1 _____

Learning Center 2 _____

Learning Center 3 _____

Learning Center 4 _____

Learning Center 5 _____

Learning Center 6 _____

Name _____

Learning Center 1 Quick Check

1. I drew a detailed picture about the story. ... **YES**   **NO**

2. I wrote a "yummy" sentence
   that tells about the story.   .... **YES**   **NO**

3. I shared my ideas with my friends. .... **YES**   **NO**

4. We shared our pictures................................ **YES**   **NO**

Learning Center 2 Quick Check

1. I can draw two (2) equal (=) lines of ants.... **YES**   **NO**

2. I can label my lines of ants with
   the correct number to show how many........ **YES**   **NO**

3. I can add my two equal lines together......... **YES**   **NO**

   I drew _____ ants in all!

Name _____

Quick
Check

1. I used these number words in my writing as a very hungry ant.

    _____   _____

2. I remembered to use punctuation
    at the end of my sentence.   .... **YES   NO**

3. My pictures match my
    words and my numbers. .... **YES   NO**

Name _____

1. There are _____ words that have four (4) letters.

2. There are _____ words that have five (5) letters.

3. There are _____ words that have six (6) letters

4. There are _____ words that have eight (8) letters.

5. The square with the MOST words is _____ .

6. The square with the LEAST words is _____ .

7. The squares with EQUAL words are

   _____ and _____ .

Name _____

1. I can draw an array of ants in this box.

2. My array has _____ ants.

3. My ants go marching _____ by _____.

Name _____

Quick
Check
✓

1. I found _____ periods (**.**) in "The Ants Go Marching."

2. I found _____ commas (**,**) in "The Ants Go Marching."

3. I found _____ exclamation marks (**!**) in "The Ants Go Marching."

4. I found _____ question marks (**?**) in "The Ants Go Marching."

Write a sentence about this song. You must use the word "ant" in your sentence. Be sure to end your sentence using the correct punctuation mark.

Name _____

Alexander, Who Used to Be Rich Last Sunday

by Judith Viorst (Author) & Ray Cruz (Illustrator)

This hilarious book is a wonderful way to teach the concept of money.

Alexander is given a dollar by his Grandma Betty and Grandpa Louie. He tries so hard to save his dollar, but there are ***so many*** things that he wants to buy. With every hilarious escapade, Alexander finds his money dwindling rather quickly.

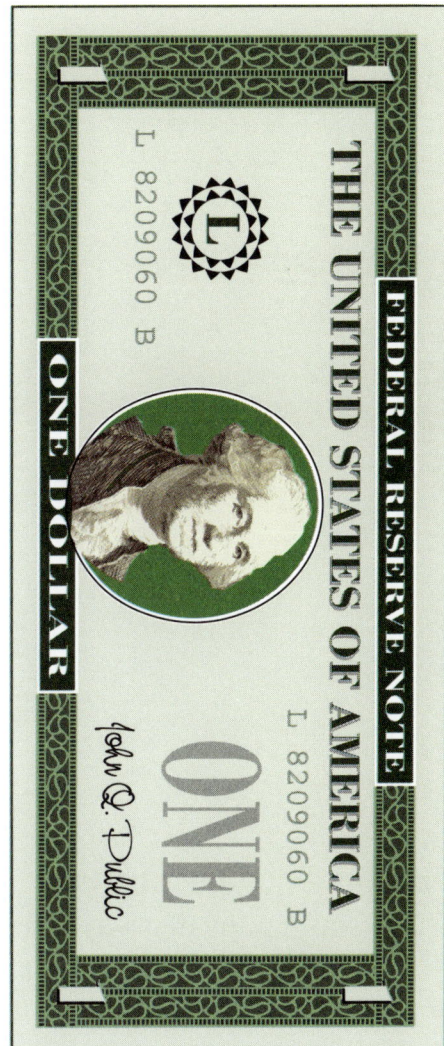

Learning Center 1
Introduction

Directions

Given three choices, students will match the correct amount of money with the correct brother and write their names—Anthony, Nicholas, and Alexander—under their choice. They will also draw the amount of money they have, then write a sentence explaining it.

Materials

- Student worksheet: Money (one per student)
- Resource page: Number words (one per student)
- Money stamps
- Pencils

Math Focus

Number and Operations
Understand numbers, ways of representing numbers, relationships among numbers, and number systems
- Connect number words and numerals to the quantities they represent, using various physical models and representations

Measurement
Understand measurable attributes of objects and the units, systems, and processes of measurement
- Recognize the attributes of length, volume, weight, area, and time
- Select an appropriate unit and tool for the attribute being measured

Apply appropriate techniques, tools, and formulas to determine measurements
- Develop common referents for measures to make comparisons and estimates

Data Analysis and Probability
Formulate questions that can be addressed with data and collect, organize, and display relevant data to answer them

Algebra
Understand patterns, relations, and functions
- Sort, classify, and order objects by size, number, and other properties

Learning Center 1

You will need these materials:
- Pencil
- Money stamps
- Money worksheet
- Number words

1. **Anthony** had two (2) dollars, three (3) quarters, one (1) dime, seven (7) nickels, and 18 pennies.

   Nicholas had one (1) dollar, two (2) quarters, five (5) dimes, five (5) nickels, and 13 pennies.

   Alexander had one (1) dollar.

2. Look at the three (3) choices of money pictured on your student worksheet. Write the correct name of each boy on the blank line next to the amount of money he had.

3. Fold your paper into fourths.
   On the back, number the top of each box.
   In box 1, stamp three (3) quarters.
   In box 2, stamp nine (9) pennies.
   In box 3, stamp five (5) dimes.
   In box 4, stamp six (6) nickels.

4. File your work and quick check, please.

Money

This amount of money belonged to _____

This amount of money belonged to _____

This amount of money belonged to _____

Name _____

Number Words

1 one	11 eleven
2 two	12 twelve
3 three	13 thirteen
4 four	14 fourteen
5 five	15 fifteen
6 six	16 sixteen
7 seven	17 seventeen
8 eight	18 eighteen
9 nine	19 nineteen
10 ten	20 twenty

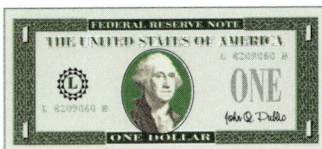

dollar   quarter dime nickel penny

Learning Center 2
Introduction

Directions

The new quarters representing
our 50 states provide an excellent
opportunity to explore the various
states. Students can copy the front
and back of a quarter and write
a sentence telling which state it
represents.

Materials

- Resource page: Circle (one per
  student, copied on card stock)
- Paper
- Pencils
- Quarters
- Scissors
- Sentence strips

Math Focus

Number and Operations
Understand numbers, ways of
representing numbers, relationships among numbers, and number
systems
- Count with understanding and
  recognize "how many" in sets of
  objects

Data Analysis
Understand and apply basic concepts of probability

Learning Center 2

You will need these materials:
- Pencils
- Scissors
- Sentence strips
- Paper
- Quarters
- Circle page

1. Cut out the circle.

2. Pick a quarter from the pile.

3. Copy the **front** of the quarter on the front of the circle.

4. Copy the **back** of the quarter on the back of the circle.

5. Copy and finish this sentence on your sentence strip.

   My quarter names the state of _____.

6. File your work and quick check, please.

Circle

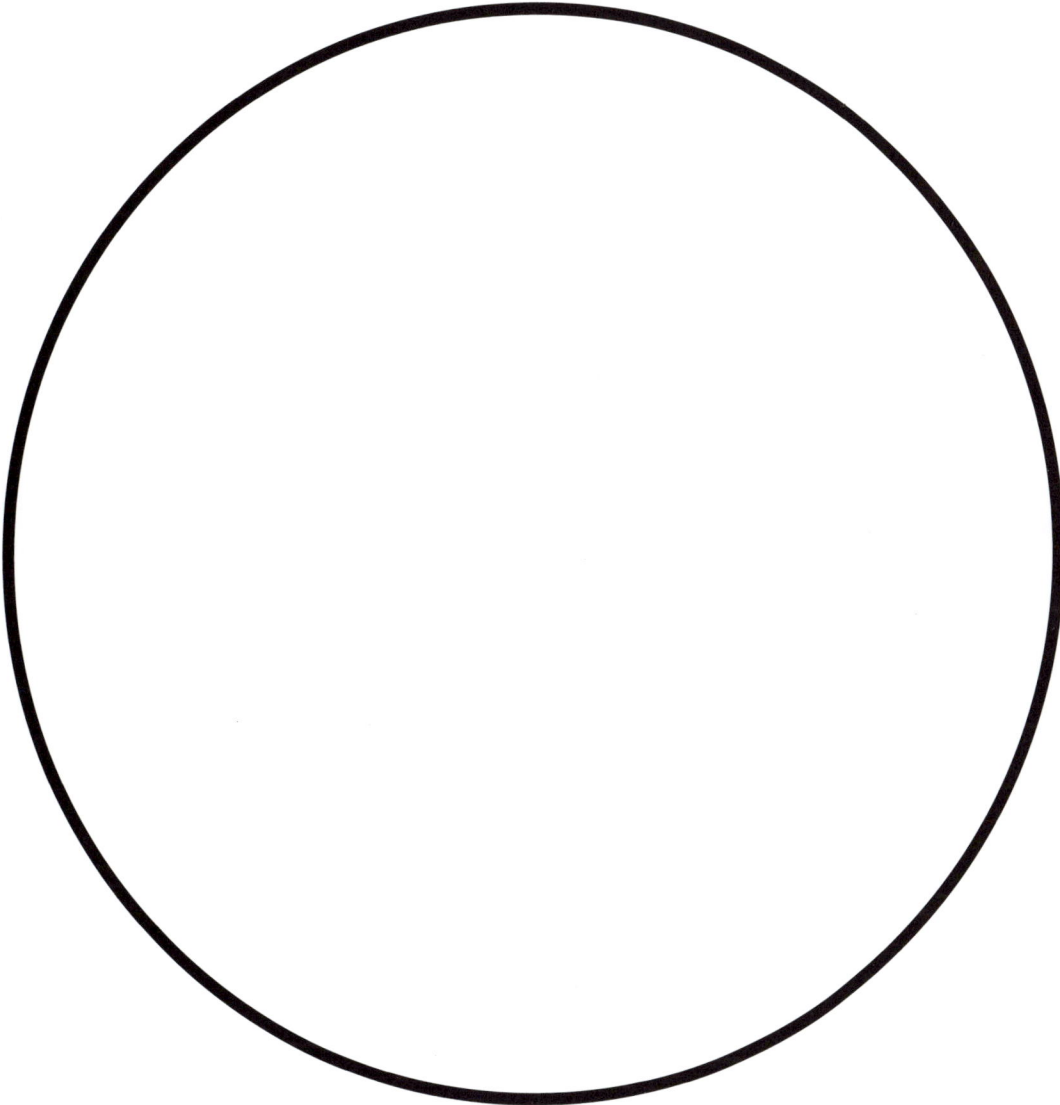

Learning Center 3
Introduction

Directions

All of us have experienced various emotions when we have spent or lost our money. On the faces worksheet, students will draw a picture of Alexander's facial expressions when: (1) he received the money from his grandpa and grandma; (2) he got fined by his dad for doing something wrong; (3) he bought the melted candle, deck of cards, and one-eyed bear; (4) he spent all his money. Students will then label the feelings under each face.

Materials

- Student worksheet: Faces (one per student)
- Crayons or markers
- Pencils

Math Focus

Number and Operations
Understand numbers, ways of representing numbers, relationships among numbers, and number systems
- Count with understanding and recognize "how many" in sets of objects

Learning Center 3

You will need these materials:
- Crayons or markers CRAYON
- Pencils
- Faces worksheet

1. In the first circle draw a picture of Alexander's face when he received one (1) dollar.

2. In the second circle draw a picture of Alexander's face when he got fined by his dad.

3. In the third circle draw a picture of Alexander's face when he bought the candle, the cards, and the one-eyed bear.

4. In the fourth circle draw a picture of Alexander's face when he spent all of his money.

5. Write the feeling to match the picture underneath each face.

6. Share your work with a friend.

7. File your work and quick check, please.

Faces

1

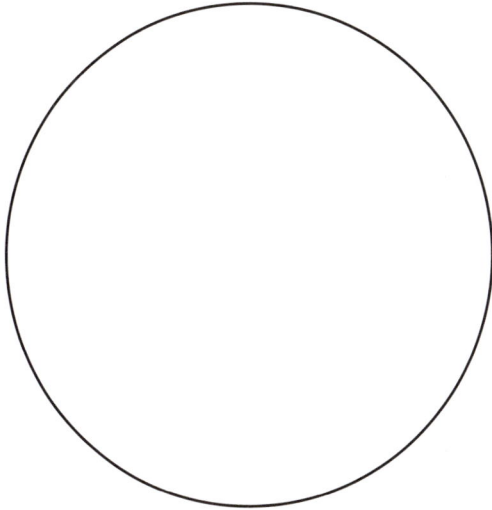

2

3

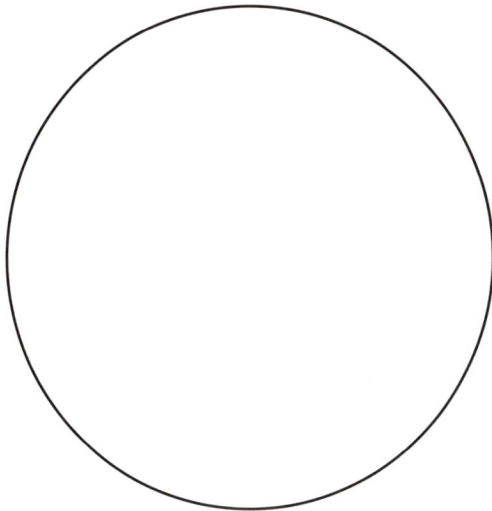

4

Name _____

Learning Center 4
Introduction

· ·

Directions

Students will create a table containing the picture, name, and value of different coins—penny, nickel, dime, and quarter.

Materials

- Resource page: Words & coins (one per student)
- Student worksheet: Money table (one per student)
- Scissors
- Glue

Math Focus

Number and Operations
Understand numbers, ways of representing numbers, relationships among numbers, and number systems
- Connect number words and numerals to the quantities they represent, using various physical models and representations

Measurement
Understand measurable attributes of objects and the units, systems, and processes of measurement
- Compare and order objects according to these attributes

Learning Center 4

You will need these materials:
- Scissors
- Glue
- Words & coins sheet
- Money table

1. Cut out the words and the coins.

2. Glue the picture, word, and value of the penny in the squares [ ] that are marked **1** on the money table.

3. Glue the picture, word, and value of the nickel in the squares [ ] that are marked **2**.

4. Glue the picture, word, and value of the dime in the squares [ ] that are marked **3**.

5. Glue the picture, word, and value of the quarter in the squares [ ] that are marked **4**.

6. File your work and quick check, please.

Money Table

1.	2.	3.	4.
1.	2.	3.	4.
1.	2.	3.	4.

Name _____

Words and Coins Sheet

nickel	quarter	dime	penny
25 cents	10 cents	1 cent	5 cents

Learning Center 5
Introduction

Directions

Here's a fun way to learn how to use a calculator. Students subtract the money that Alexander spends and record the amounts as the money dwindles away.

Materials

- Calculators
  (one per student)
- Student worksheet: Good-bye money (one per student, copy two-sided)
- Pencils

Math Focus

Number and Operations
Compute fluently and make reasonable estimates
- Use a variety of methods and tools to compute, including objects, mental computation, estimation, paper and pencil, and calculators

Algebra
Represent and analyze mathematical situations and structures using algebraic symbols
- Use concrete, pictorial, and verbal representations to develop an understanding of invented and conventional symbolic notations

Learning Center 5

You will need these materials:
- Pencil
- Good-bye money sheet
- Calculator

1. Follow the directions on the good-bye money sheet.

2. Can you find ▬ on your calculator?

3. Can you find ═ on your calculator?

4. Can you find • on your calculator?

5. Can you find numbers 1 2 4 5 6 on your calculator?

6. Check your work with a friend.

7. File your work and quick check, please.

Good-bye Money

1. Grandma Betty and Grandpa Louie gave me a dollar.

   Press 1.00 on your calculator.

2. I went to the store and bought bubble gum. **Bubble Gum**
   Good-bye 15 cents.

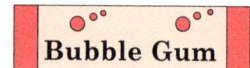

   Press -.15 = on your calculator. Record _____

3. I bet that I could hold my breath to a count of 300, but I couldn't. *Good-bye 15 cents.*

   Press -.15 = on your calculator. Record _____

4. I rented Eddie's snake. *Good-bye 12 cents.*

   Press -.12 = on your calculator. Record _____

5. I got fined for saying bad words to my brother. *Good-bye 10 cents.*

   Press -.10 = on your calculator. Record _____

6. I lost eight (8) cents. *Good-bye eight (8) cents.*

   Press -.08 = on your calculator. Record _____

7. I ate Anthony's smushed candy bar. *Good-bye 11 cents.*

   Press -.11 = on your calculator. Record _____

8. Nicholas performed a magic trick and made my money disappear. *Good-bye 4 cents.*

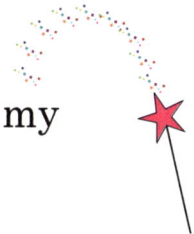

   Press -.04 = on your calculator. Record _____

9. I kicked Nicholas and got fined by my dad. *Good-bye 5 cents.*

   Press -.05 = on your calculator. Record _____

10. I bought a melted candle, cards, and a one-eyed bear. *Good-bye 20 cents.*

   Press -.20 = on your calculator. Record _____

   After all that, I have _____ left!

Name _____

Learning Center 6
Introduction

Directions

There is no better method for learning about money than by going to the store to buy something. Students will each be given 10 pennies to go to the store to purchase different priced items to decorate Nicholas's magic hat. After decorating the hat, they will write a sentence about a trick they would perform as a magician. Remind students to start with a capital letter and end with a period.

Materials

- Crayons
- 10 pennies for each child
- Small paper cups to hold pennies
- Items for decorating hats such as feathers, stickers, sequins, buttons, cut up tissue paper, etc.
- Index cards to mark cost of items (e.g., one feather for one penny, three stickers for one penny, five sequins for one penny, etc.)
- Resource page: Hat (one per student)
- Sentence strips
- Glue
- Stapler

Math Focus

Number and Operations
Understand numbers, ways of representing numbers, relationships among numbers, and number systems
- Count with understanding and recognize "how many" in sets of objects

Learning Center 6

You will need these materials:
- Pencil
- Glue
- Sentence strip
- Crayons
- 10 pennies
- Magic hat page
- Stapler
- Decorations

1. Go to the store and buy items to decorate your magic hat.

2. Spend your ten (10) pennies.

3. Think about how to decorate your magic hat.

4. Glue the decorations on your magic hat.

5. Copy and finish this sentence on your sentence strip:

    _____ can make a _____ disappear.
        Name

    Make sure you use correct capitalization and punctuation.

6. Staple the sentence strip to your magic hat.

7. File your work and quick check, please.

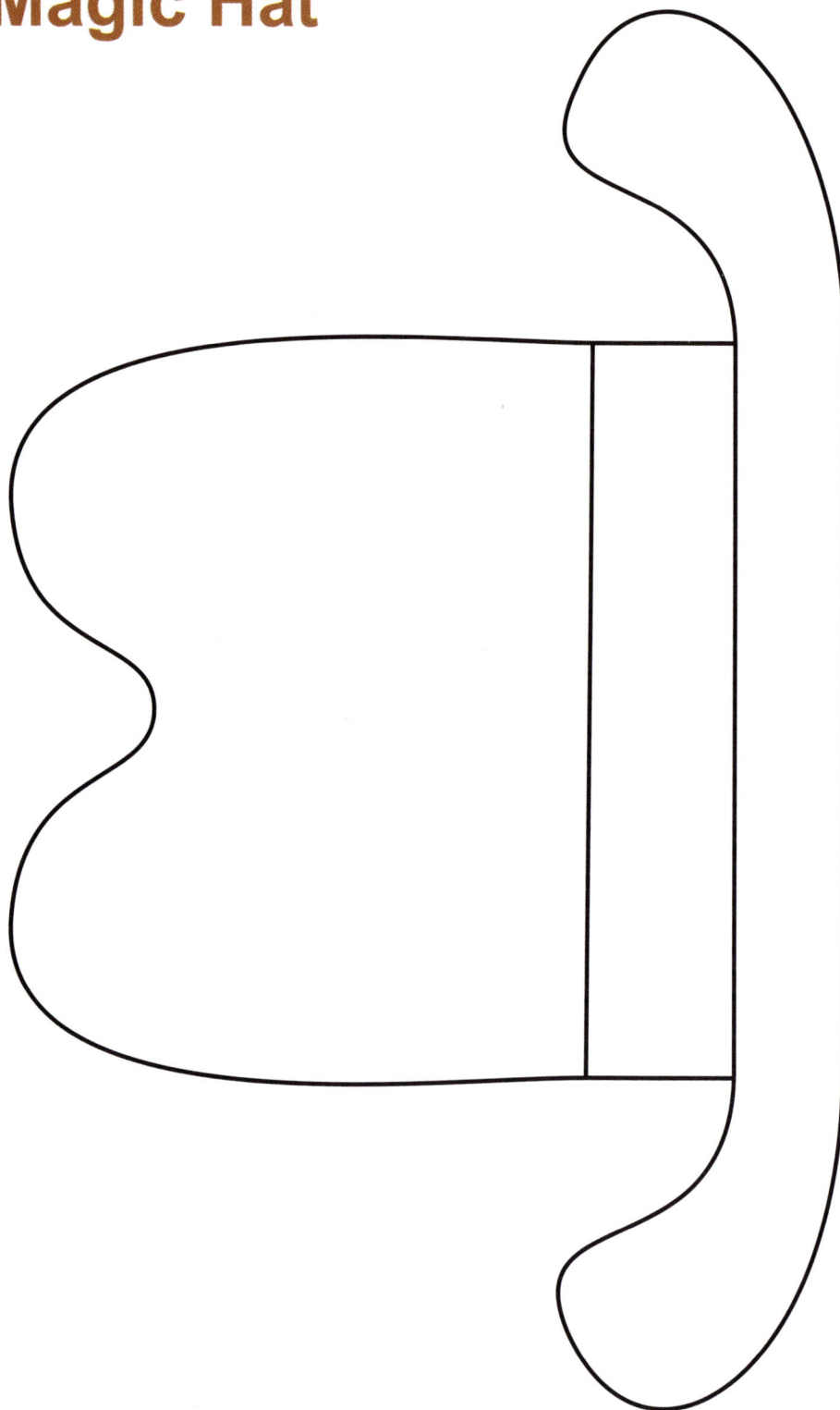

Magic Hat

Alexander, Who Used to Be Rich Last Sunday

Learning Center 1 _____

Learning Center 2 _____

Learning Center 3 _____

Learning Center 4 _____

Learning Center 5 _____

Learning Center 6 _____

Name _____

1.   If I had a dollar, I would buy_____

_____

Name   _____

Learning Center 2 Quick Check

Take your quarter and throw it in the air ten (10) times. Did it come up heads or tails? Make a tally mark (|) on the line for heads or for tails each time you toss it.

1.   Tally marks for **heads**: _____

      Total number of heads: _____

2.   Tally marks for **tails**: _____

      Total number of tails: _____

Name   _____

Learning Center 3 Quick Check

1.   Which of the coins is your favorite? _____

2.   Why? _____

Name _____

Learning Center 4 Quick Check

Sort all of the coins that are in your tub on each plate.

1.   Record the number of pennies. _____

2.   Record the number of nickels. _____

3.   Record the number of dimes. _____

4.   Record the number of quarters. _____

5.   I had the most _____. I had the least _____.

Name _____

Learning Center 5 Quick Check ✔ Quick Check

1.   What can you do with a calculator? _____

2.   I had fun using the calculator.   **Yes   No**

Name _____

Learning Center 6 Quick Check ✔ Quick Check

1.   I bought _____ _____.
         how many   item

2.   I bought _____ _____.
         how many   item

3.   I bought _____ _____.
         how many   item

4.   I bought _____ _____.
         how many   item

5.   I spent _____ cents.

Name _____

Chicka Chicka 1, 2, 3

by Bill Martin, Jr. (Author), Michael Sampson (Author), & Lois Ehlert (Illustrator)

● ●

1 told 2 and 2 told 3, "I'll race you to the top of the apple tree."

Seeing numbers race up the trunk of the apple tree is no surprise. But, what about poor Zero? He is left behind, hiding in the corner. The numbers race up the tree, by ones and 10s, and race down again, counting forward as they go up the tree and counting backward as they make their way down. As the numbers are threatened by a swarm of bumblebees, Zero saves the day and becomes the HERO. He joins 10 at the top of the tree where he turns into 100!

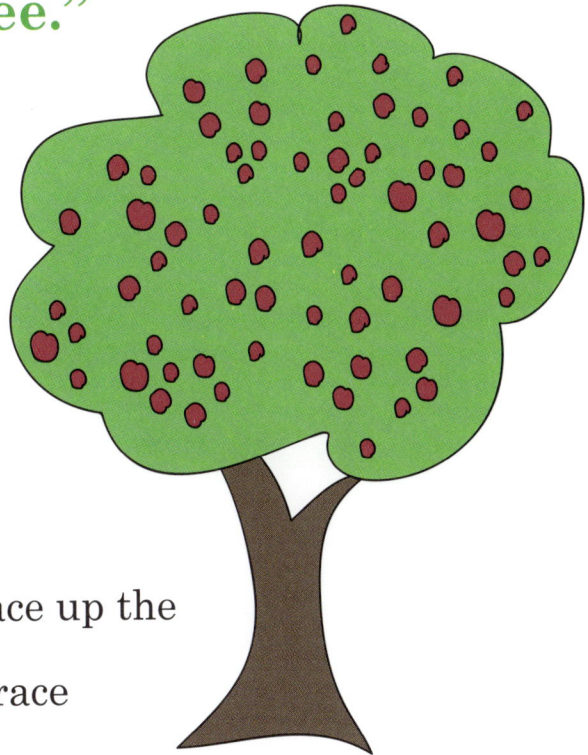

Learning Center 1
Introduction

Directions

The students will demonstrate their ability to write numbers correctly and creatively as they illustrate a story, integrating numbers into their pictures. Ones become blades of grass, eights become butterflies—the ideas are endless!

Materials

- Drawing paper
- Crayons
- Number lines
  (one per student)
- Copy of the book
  (one per student)
- Listening center tape of *Chicka Chicka 1, 2, 3* and earphones
  (one per student)

Math Focus

Number and Operations
Understand numbers, ways of representing numbers, relationships among numbers, and number systems
- Develop a sense of whole numbers and represent and use them in flexible ways, including relating, composing, and decomposing numbers

Learning Center 1

You will need these materials:
- Crayons
- Number line
- Drawing paper
- *Chicka Chicka 1, 2, 3*
- Earphones

1. You will work at the listening center.
   Listen to the story from beginning to end.
   Follow along in your book.
   Be sure to look at the pictures!

2. Draw a picture showing a surprise!
   Use numbers to create your picture.
   Here are some ideas:

   Zero (0) is the sun!
   The sun's rays are sevens (7)!
   Grass is made of ones (1)!

3. Be sure to use lots of different colored crayons.

4. Share your picture with a friend.

5. File your work and quick check, please.

Learning Center 2
Introduction

Directions

The students will measure and mark an apple tree by 10s to show their knowledge of number order and progression. Students will then draw a picture showing Zero the Hero at the end of the story.

Materials

- Student worksheet: Apple tree (one per student)
- Number line (by 10s, one per student) or number poster
- Pencils
- Crayons
- *Chicka Chicka 1, 2, 3* (one per student)

Math Focus

Numbers and Operations

Understand numbers, ways of representing numbers, relationships among numbers, and number systems

- Use multiple models to develop initial understanding of place value and the base-10 number system
- Develop a sense of whole numbers and represent and use them in flexible ways, including relating, composing, and decomposing numbers

Learning Center 2

You will need these materials:

- Pencil
- Crayons
- Number line `10 20 30 40 50 60`
- *Chicka Chicka 1,2,3*
- Apple tree

Book

1. Use the book, Book a number line, `10 20 30 40 50 60` or a poster to help you count and write the numbers by 10s in the circles ( ) all the way up the tree.

2. Check your work. Read the numbers by 10s to a friend.

   Front Back

   Turn your apple tree paper over.

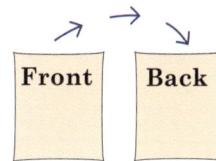

3. Using crayons, CRAYON draw a picture showing zero (**0**) at the end of the story.

4. Write a sentence with a pencil to tell about your picture.

5. File your work and quick check, please. Quick Check ✓

Apple Tree

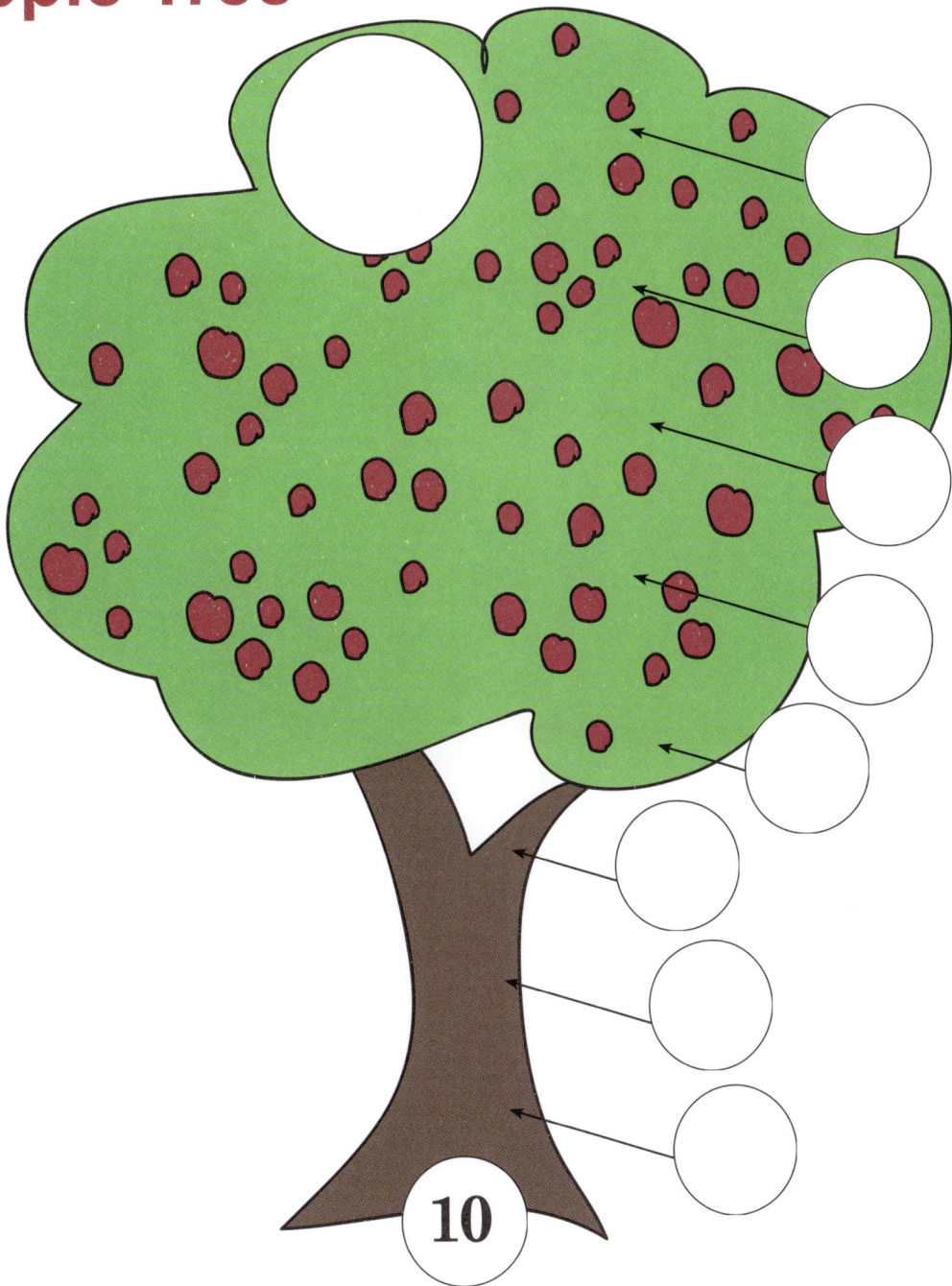

Can you take **Zero the Hero** up the tree? Count by 10s and write the numbers in the circles.

Name _____

Learning Center 3
Introduction

Directions

If Zero the Hero could talk, what would he say? Students will use a paper plate to create a Zero puppet. They will act out the story as they retell it. Finally, they will write their own story as if they were Zero the Hero who has just saved the day!

Materials

- Paper plate with center removed (one per student)
- Scissors
- Craft sticks (one per student)
- Tape
- Crayons (five per student)
- Pencils
- Yarn, sequins, paper strips, ribbon (10 per student)
- Buttons (two per student)
- Student worksheet: Bubbles (one per student)
- *Chicka Chicka 1, 2, 3* (one per student)

Math Focus

Number and Operations

Understand numbers, ways of representing numbers, relationships among numbers, and number systems

- Count with understanding and recognize "how many" in sets of objects

Learning Center 3

You will need these materials:

- Pencil
- Scissors
- Tape
- One (1) paper plate
- One (1) stick
- Two (2) buttons to decorate your Zero the Hero puppet

- *Chicka Chicka 1, 2, 3*
- Glue
- Bubble paper
- Five (5) crayons
- Ten (10) scraps

1. Create a Zero the Hero puppet. Be sure to share art supplies with your friends at your center.

2. Pretend you are Zero. Use the book *Chicka Chicka 1, 2, 3* to read and tell the story using a happy voice. Now try reading it in a sad voice. Can you read in a jealous voice?

3. Use the bubble sheet to write what you think Zero would be saying. Use your Zero the Hero Puppet speaking voice when you share what you've written with your friends.

4. File your work and quick check, please.

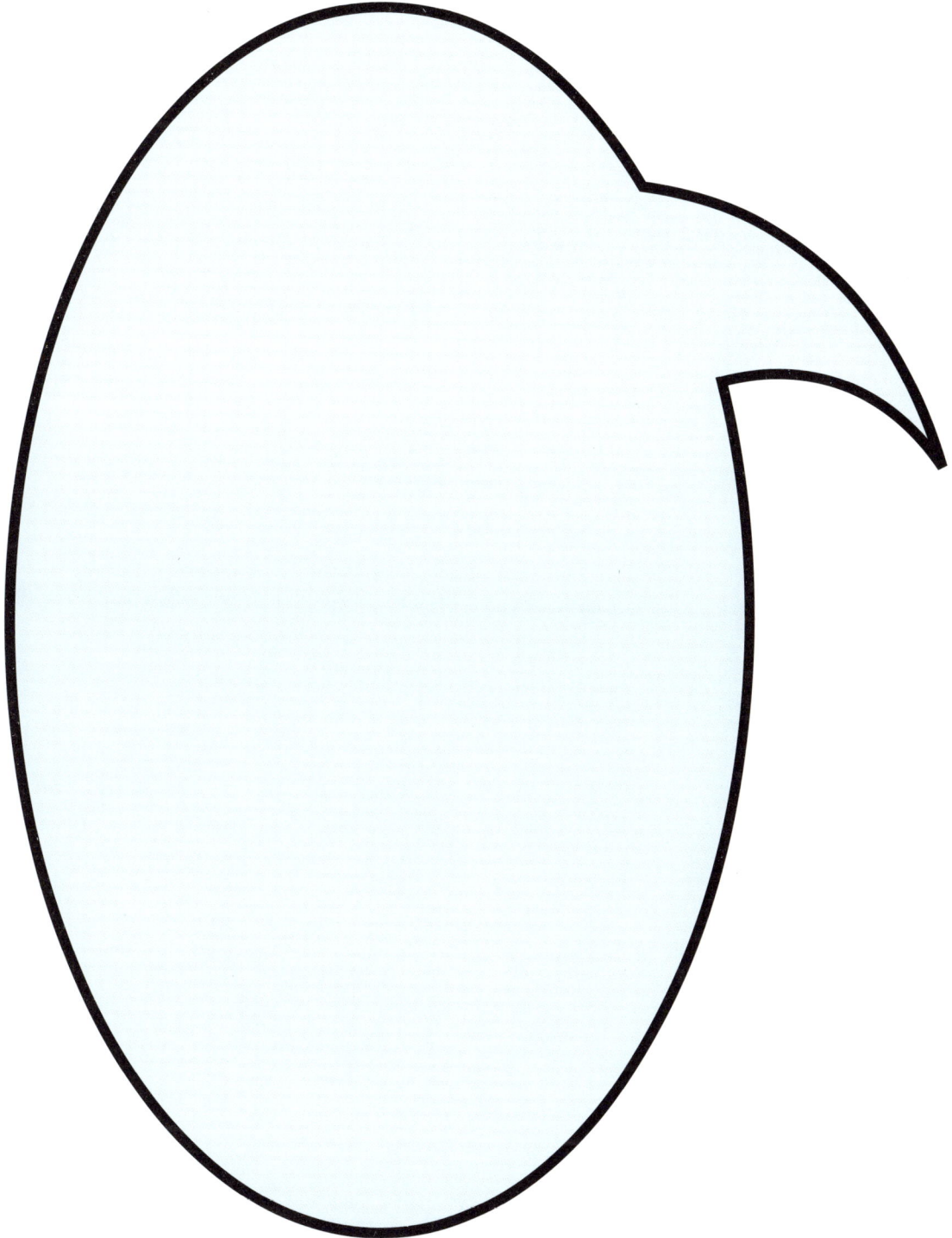

Bubble

Name _____

Learning Center 4
Introduction

Directions

Students will begin to recognize the number words ten, twenty, thirty, and on to one hundred by completing a simple matching sheet. Then, choosing four favorite number words, they will write sentences to represent their understanding of each number and complete an illustration.

Materials

- Student worksheet: 10s matching page (one per student)
- Student worksheet: Four-box sheet (one per student)
- Pencils
- Crayons
- 10s poster
- Number books

Math Focus

Connections
Recognize and apply mathematics in contexts outside of math

Number and Operations
Understand numbers, ways of representing numbers, relationships among numbers, and number systems
- Count with understanding and recognize "how many" in sets of objects
- Use multiple models to develop initial understandings of place value and the base-10 number system
- Connect number words and numerals to the quantities they represent, using various physical models and representations

Representation
Create and use representations to organize, record, and communicate mathematical ideas

Learning Center 4

You will need these materials:
- Pencil
- Crayons
- Matching page
- Number books at the center
- 10s poster that is in our room
- Four-box sheet

1. Match the numbers to the words on the matching page. Use the classroom 10s poster to help you. Use a pencil. Be sure to check your work!

2. Choose any four (4) number words you like.

3. Use the four-box sheet that looks like this:

4. In each box, write a sentence using one (1) of the number words. Draw a picture about it. Use the number books at the center to give you some great ideas.

    Here is an example of a super sentence:
    There are twenty (20) cheerful children in our class.

5. File your work and quick check, please.

10s Matching

thirty	40
fifty	10
sixty	90
ten	70
seventy	30
ninety	20
twenty	80
forty	50
sixty	60

Name _____

Four-Box Worksheet

1	2
3	4

Name _____

Learning Center 5
Introduction

Directions

The students will cut and paste a scrambled phrase from the story on a sentence strip.

Materials

- Resource page: Word page (one per student)
- Scissors
- Glue
- Pencils
- Sentence strips

Math Focus

Algebra

Understand patterns, relations, and functions
- Sort, classify, and order objects by size, number, and other properties

Number and Operations

Understand numbers, ways of representing numbers, relationships among numbers, and number systems
- Count with understanding and recognize "how many" in sets of objects

Learning Center 5

You will need these materials:

- Pencil
- Scissors
- Word page

- Glue
- Sentence strip

1. Cut the words apart. They are scrambled on the page.

2. Line the words up on the sentence strip in the correct order.

3. Read them to a friend or to yourself. Does the sentence make sense?

4. Glue each word in the correct order.

5. Does your sentence say this?

   Chicka Chicka 1, 2, 3 ... Will there be a place for me?

6. Who do you think is speaking? Write your answer on the sentence strip.

7. File your work and quick check, please.

Word Page

me	place	”
?	Chicka	1,
Will	for	3...
Chicka	there	a
be	2,	“

Learning Center 6
Introduction

Directions

Count the words! Students will write about the story, *Chicka Chicka 1, 2, 3*. Using high-frequency words and the book to help them, the students will write a letter to a friend recommending this story.

Materials

- Student worksheet: Letter
  (one per student)
- Resource page: Most-used words
  (one per student)
- Pencils
- Crayons
- Cup with name slips of each
  student in the class
- *Chicka Chicka 1, 2, 3*
  (one per student)

Math Focus

Numbers and Operations

Understand numbers, ways of representing numbers, relationships among numbers, and number systems

- Count with understanding and recognize "how many" in sets of objects

Learning Center 6

You will need these materials:
- Pencil
- Crayons
- *Chicka Chicka 1, 2, 3*
- Letter
- Most-used words

1. Pick the name of a classroom friend from the cup.

2. Using a pencil, you will write a letter to that friend about the book *Chicka Chicka 1, 2, 3*.

3. Use the word list to help you write.

4. Try your best to write five (5) interesting sentences, or use thirty (30) very wonderful words in your letter. Remember to use a period, (.) or a question mark, (?) or an exclamation mark (!) at the end of your sentences. Also, remember to use commas (,).

5. Draw a picture to illustrate your letter. Use crayons and colorful details.

6. Be sure to write your name at the end of the letter.

7. File your work and quick check, please.

Letter

Date _____

Dear _____ ,

_____

_____

_____

_____

_____

Your friend,

_____

Most-Used Words

1. the	18. his	35. where
2. of	19. they	36. we
3. and	20. I	37. when
4. a	21. at	38. your
5. to	22. be	39. can
6. in	23. this	40. said
7. is	24. have	41. there
8. you	25. from	42. use
9. that	26. or	43. an
10. it	27. one	44. each
11. he	28. had	45. which
12. was	29. by	46. she
13. for	30. word	47. do
14. on	31. but	48. how
15. are	32. not	49. their
16. as	33. what	50. if
17. with	34. all	

Chicka Chicka 1, 2, 3

Learning Center 1 _____

Learning Center 2 _____

Learning Center 3 _____

Learning Center 4 _____

Learning Center 5 _____

Learning Center 6 _____

Name _____

Learning Center 1 Quick Check

1. Make a list of the numbers that you used in your illustration. List the numbers only one (1) time, please.

_____

_____

2. Here's a challenge! What numbers did you NOT use in your picture? List the numbers only one (1) time, please.

_____

Name _____

1. What number do you see **first,** at the bottom of the tree?

    _____

2. What number do you see **fifth,** in the middle of the tree?

    _____

3. What number do you see **last,** at the top of the tree?

    _____

4. Can you count **backward** from ten (10)?

    10, _____

Name _____

Learning Center 3 Quick Check

1. I read *Chicka Chicka 1, 2, 3* in a _____ voice.

happy   sad   jealous

2. Draw a picture in this circle to show your voice.

Name _____

1. Write the numbers that match these words. Use our classroom posters and your paper from the center to help you.

   ten _____ eighty _____ sixty _____ thirty _____

   twenty _____ fifty _____ seventy _____

   forty _____ ninety _____ one hundred _____

2. What number is your favorite? _____

Name _____

Quick
Check

1.   Count the number of words in this sentence:

      "Chicka Chicka 1, 2, 3. . . Will there be a place for me?"

      Write the number of words here: _____

2.   Do you remember if there is room for Zero in the tree?

      _____ Yes, there is room for Zero in the tree.

      _____ No, there is no room for Zero in the tree.

Name _____

1.   I wrote my letter to _____ .

2.   I wrote the date at the top of the letter.   **YES**   **NO**

3.   I signed my name at the end of the letter.   **YES**   **NO**

4.   I drew a picture with crayons
     about the story for my friend.   **YES**   **NO**

Name _____

The Doorbell Rang

by Pat Hutchins

• •

Ma baked twelve cookies for her children.

Each child gets six cookies until the doorbell rings. Two more children come and now there are three cookies for each until the doorbell rings again. Four more children come and now there are two cookies for each child. As the doorbell keeps ringing, the children get fewer and fewer cookies. This book teaches sharing equally in a wonderful and creative fashion and is an excellent tool for teaching prediction and simple division.

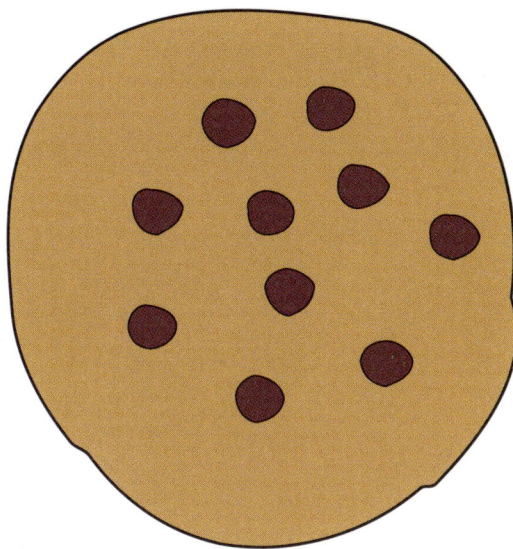

Learning Center 1
Introduction

. . . .

Directions

What other foods could the children in the story share besides cookies? Students will fold a paper into fourths. In each quarter of the paper, they will draw and label a different food that could be shared with other children. This could be used as a good introduction to fractions if some of the foods are easily divisible such as pies, loaves of bread, or bananas.

Materials

- Paper
- Crayons
- Pencils

Math Focus

Number and Operations
Understand numbers, ways of representing numbers, relationships among numbers, and number systems
- Count with understanding and recognize "how many" in sets of objects
- Develop a sense of whole numbers and represent and use them in flexible ways, including relating, composing, and decomposing numbers
- Understand and represent commonly used fractions such as 1/4, 1/3, and 1/2.

Learning Center 1

You will need these materials:
- Crayons
- Pencils
- Paper

1. Take one paper and fold it in half, hot dog style.

2. Take the paper and fold it again in fourths, hamburger style.

3. Open your paper. Number each fourth.

4. Write your name on your paper.

5. In each square, draw a different food that you could share. Label each food.

6. File your work and quick check, please.

Learning Center 2
Introduction

Directions

Students will create their own cookie recipe with the help of a teacher/assistant to record ingredients, baking utensils, and steps. Be prepared for some CRAZY recipes!

This is an ideal time to introduce measuring tools used in cooking. An extra special treat is to provide chocolate chip cookies for students when they are finished with their recipes.

Materials

- Chart paper
- Markers
- A variety of measuring tools used in the kitchen
- Chocolate chip cookies (optional)

Math Focus

Number and Operations

Understand numbers, ways of representing numbers, relationships among numbers, and number systems
- Develop understanding of the relative position and magnitude of whole numbers and of ordinal and cardinal numbers and their connections

Measurement

Understand measurable attributes of objects and the units, systems, and processes of measurement
- Recognize the attributes of length, volume, weight, area, and time
- Select an appropriate unit and tool for the attribute being measured

Representation

Create and use representations to organize, record, and communicate mathematical ideas

Learning Center 2

You will need the help of a teacher or adult and these materials:

• Markers ——marker——   • Paper [BIG]

1. Your group will write a recipe for chocolate chip cookies. Take turns and tell your teacher/helper the ingredients that you will need for your cookies. She will write ——marker—— it on chart paper. [BIG]

2. Take turns and tell your teacher/helper the first step in making the batter for your cookies. Tell your teacher/helper the second step and then the third step.

3. How hot does the oven need to be?

    How long will you bake the cookies?

4. Take turns and read your recipe.

5. Fill out your quick check and file, please.

Learning Center 3
Introduction

Directions

Decorating cookies is lots of fun and can also be a learning experience. Using paper circles, squares, rectangles, and triangles, students will glue a face on a paper cookie. Students will then write a sentence describing the expression on their cookie face.

Materials

- Round cookie shape on brown card stock (one per student)
- Circle, square, rectangle, and triangle paper shapes
- Crayons
- Glue
- Pencils
- Sentence strips (one per student)

Math Focus

Number and Operations
Understand numbers, ways of representing numbers, relationships among numbers, and number systems
- Count with understanding and recognize "how many" in sets of objects

Geometry
Analyze characteristics and properties of two- and three-dimensional geometric shapes and develop mathematical arguments about geometric relationships
- Recognize, name, build, draw, compare, and sort two- and three-dimensional shapes

Learning Center 3

You will need these materials:
- Crayons
- Pencil
- One (1) cookie shape
- Paper shapes:

Circles   Squares

Rectangles   Triangles

1. Create a face on your paper cookie using the shapes: circle, square, rectangle, and triangle.

   Glue the shapes on the cookie.

2. What expression is on your cookie face?
   Copy and finish this sentence on the sentence strip:

   My cookie face is _____ .

3. File your work and quick check, please.

Learning Center 4
Introduction

Directions

Students will be introduced to less than, more than, least, most, and equal. To demonstrate their understanding of these words, students will draw cookies on plates to show less than, more than, and equal. They will pick a plate of cookies with the most and the least amount of cookies.

Materials

- Crayons
- Pencils
- Student worksheet: Cookie sheet (one per student)

Math Focus

Number and Operations

Understand numbers, ways of representing numbers, relationships among numbers, and number systems
- Count with understanding and recognize "how many" in sets of objects
- Develop understanding of the relative position and magnitude of whole numbers and of ordinal and cardinal numbers and their connections
- Develop a sense of whole numbers and represent and use them in flexible ways, including relating, composing, and decomposing numbers

Understand meanings of operations and how they relate to one another
- Understand various meanings of addition and subtraction of whole numbers and the relationship between the two operations

Learning Center 4

You will need these materials:
- Crayons
- Pencil

- Cookie sheet

1. On the cookie sheet, look at the first set of two circles ◯◯ and draw cookies 🍪 to show less than. (**<**)

2. On your second set of two circles ◯◯ draw cookies 🍪 to show more than. (**>**)

3. On your third set of two circles ◯◯ draw cookies 🍪 to show equal. (**=**)

4. Look at the first set of three (3) circles. ◯◯◯ Count and write the number of cookies 🍪 under each plate. Find the plate of cookies 🍪 that has the **MOST** and label it on the plate under the cookies.

5. Look at the second set of three (3) circles. ◯◯◯ Count and write the number of cookies 🍪 under each plate. Find the plate of cookies 🍪 that has the **LEAST** and label it in the plate under the cookies.

6. File your work and quick check, please.

Cookie Sheet

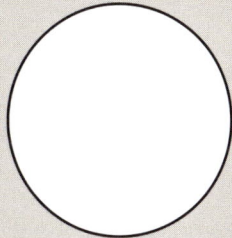 less than <

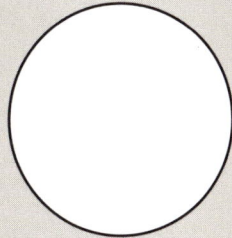 more than >

 equal =

 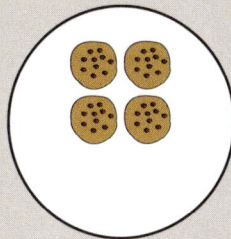 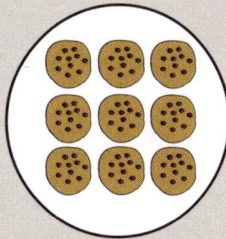

_____   _____   _____ Number

_____   _____   _____ Label

 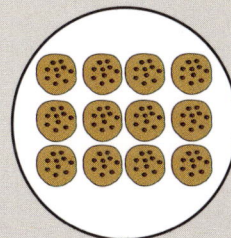 

_____   _____   _____ Number

_____   _____   _____ Label

Name

Learning Center 5
Introduction

Directions

The Doorbell Rang is a great introduction to the concept of division. The students will cut out 12 cookies and 12 children. Using the manipulatives, the students will arrange their cookies and children to demonstrate how to divide the cookies equally, according to the number of children: 2, 4, 6, and 12. They will record their answers on the worksheets.

Materials

- Resource page: Cookie sheet (one per student)
- Resource page: Children (one per student)
- Student worksheet: Number sentences (one per student)
- Scissors
- Pencils
- Zipping plastic bags (one per student)
- Work space (table, etc.)

Math Focus

Number and Operations

Understand numbers, ways of representing numbers, relationships among numbers, and number systems
- Count with understanding and recognize "how many" in sets of objects

Understand meanings of operations and how they relate to one another
- Understand situations that entail multiplication and division, such as equal groupings of objects and sharing equally

Compute fluently and make reasonable estimates
- Develop and use strategies for whole-number computations, with a focus on addition and subtraction
- Use a variety of methods and tools to compute, including objects, mental computation, estimation, paper and pencil, and calculators

Learning Center 5

You will need these materials:
- Pencil
- Scissors
- Work space
- Zipping plastic bag
- Sheet of cookies
- Sheet of children
- Number sentence sheet

1. Cut out the twelve (12) cookies and twelve (12) children. Sort them into two (2) piles.

2. Put two (2) children on your work space. Place an equal (=) number of cookies on your work space below the two (2) children. Record the number of cookies on your worksheet. Return your children and cookies to their piles.

3. Put four (4) children on your work space. Place an equal (=) number of cookies on your work space below the four (4) children. Record the number of cookies on your worksheet. Return your children and cookies to their piles.

4. Put six (6) children on your work space. Place an equal (=) number of cookies on your space and record.

5. Put twelve (12) children on your work space. Place an equal (=) number of cookies on your work space and record.

6. Store children and cookies in zipping plastic bags to show at home.

7. File your work and quick check, please.

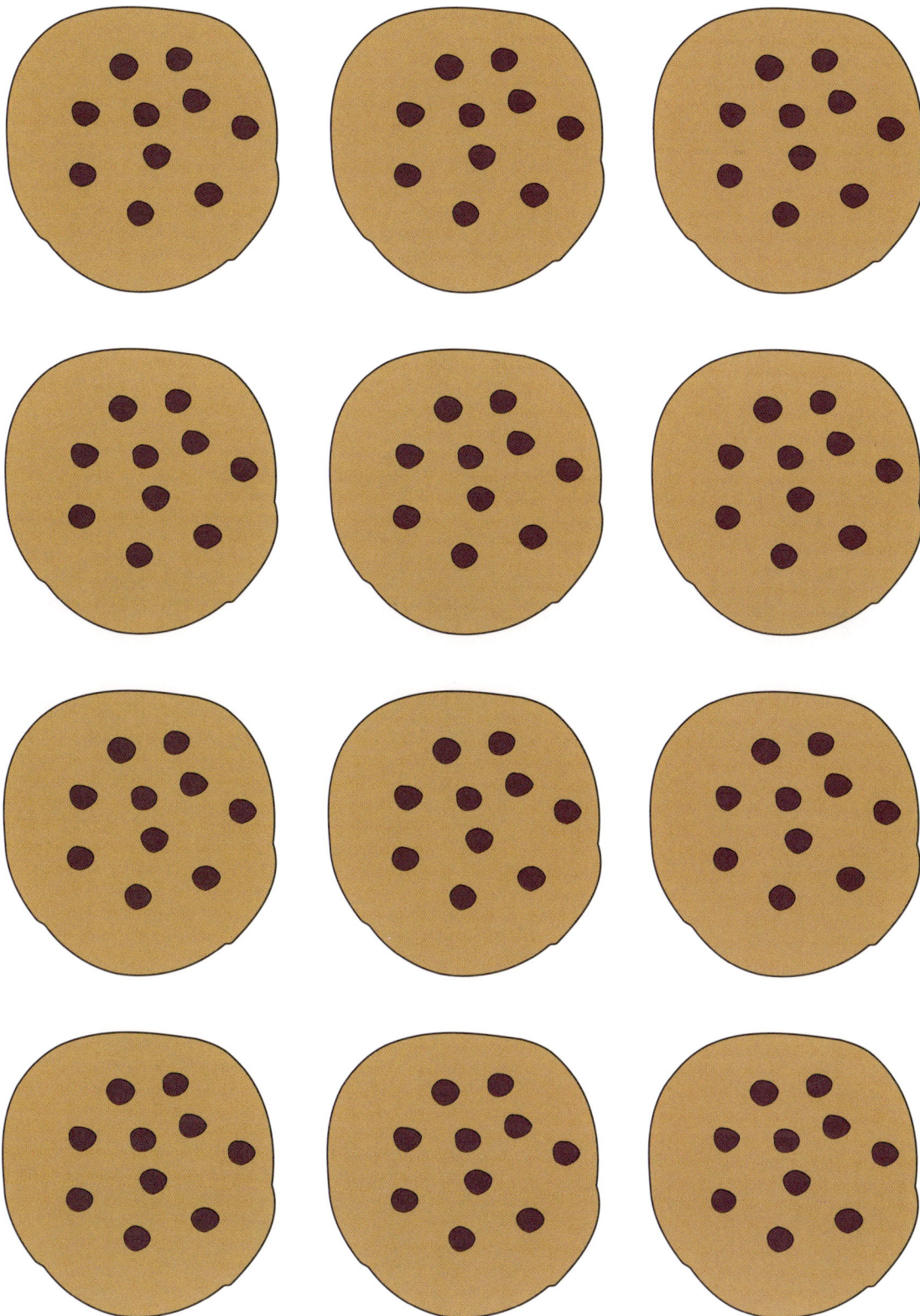

Cookies

Children

Number Sentences

Write the number sentences that you made:

_____ + _____ = 12

As the doorbell rang.

_____ + _____ + _____ + _____ = 12

As the doorbell rang.

___ + ___ + ___ + ___ + ___ + ___ = 12

As the doorbell rang.

____ + ____ + ____ + ____ + ____ +

____ + ____ + ____ + ____ + ____ +

____ + ____ = 12

As the doorbell rang.

Name _____

Learning Center 6
Introduction

Directions

There is great dialogue in *The Doorbell Rang* to introduce children to quotation marks. Students will count and record the number of sets of quotation marks on eight marked pages. (This counts as one set—" ".) The teacher will mark the eight pages with sticky notes or paper clip flags and number them prior to class.

Materials

- *The Doorbell Rang*
  (one per student)
- Student worksheet: Quotations
  (one per student)
- Pencils
- Sticky notes or paper clip flags

Math Focus

Number and Operations
Understand numbers, ways of representing numbers, relationships among numbers and number systems
- Count with understanding and recognize "how many" in sets of objects
- Develop understanding of the relative position and magnitude of whole numbers and of ordinal and cardinal numbers and their connections

Learning Center 6

You will need these materials:
- Pencil
- *The Doorbell Rang*
- Quotations sheet

1. Read the book and look for quotation marks " " that show when people are talking.

2. Count the number of sets of quotation marks " " on page 1. Write the number on your worksheet.

3. Count the number of sets of quotation marks " " on page 2. Write the number on your worksheet.

4. Continue until you have finished all eight (8) pages.

5. Look at your student worksheet. Which page had the **MOST** quotation marks " " ? Write the page number on your worksheet.

6. Look at your student worksheet. Which page had the **FEWEST** quotation marks " " ? Write the page number on your worksheet.

7. File your worksheet and quick check, please.

Quotations

Page 1 has _____ sets of " " marks.

Page 2 has _____ sets of " " marks.

Page 3 has _____ sets of " " marks.

Page 4 has _____ sets of " " marks.

Page 5 has _____ sets of " " marks.

Page 6 has _____ sets of " " marks.

Page 7 has _____ sets of " " marks.

Page 8 has _____ sets of " " marks.

Which page had the **MOST** sets? _____

Which page had the **FEWEST** sets? ____

Name _____

The Doorbell Rang

Learning Center 1 _____

Learning Center 2 _____

Learning Center 3 _____

Learning Center 4 _____

Learning Center 5 _____

Learning Center 6 _____

Name _____

1. Write the number of cookies in each set. Circle the set that has **MORE** cookies.

    _____   _____

2. Write the number of cookies in each set. Circle the set that has **MORE** cookies.

    _____   _____

3. Draw your own set of cookies below. Write the number to show how many are in your set.

Name _____

Quick
Check ✔

1. Circle the measuring tools that you would use to bake chocolate chip cookies.

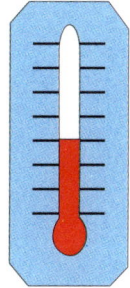

Name _____

Learning Center 3 Quick Check

Quick
Check ✔

1. I used _____ circles.

2. I used _____ squares.

3. I used _____ triangles.

4. I used _____ rectangles.

Name _____

Quick Check

1. Draw cookies to show three (3) number sentences. Label them.

Example: 4   +   2   =   6

Name _____

1. Write your own sentence about children and cookies.

2. Draw children and cookies to show your sentence.

3. Make sure each child gets an equal (=) number of cookies.

Name _____

Quick
Check

✓

1. Write a sentence using quotation marks " " .

_____

_____

_____

_____

_____

_____

_____

_____

Name _____

Each Orange Had 8 Slices

by Paul Giganti, Jr. (Author) & Donald Crews (Illustrator)

In this wonderfully colorful book

every child will find

something to add,

multiply, or count.

Numbers abound in

our world, and this

book encourages us

to look, to see, to count,

and to discover.

Open the pages...

get started...

one, two, three, *COUNT!*

Learning Center 1
Introduction

Directions

Creative ideas and detailed colorful
pictures will challenge students to
think of a new place or a new object
and begin the process of counting
"how many" of their own objects,
parts, or pieces. The class book
they produce is sure to become a
favorite!

Materials
- *Each Orange Had 8 Slices*
  (one per student)
- Pencils
- Crayons
- Student worksheet: What I saw
- Drawing paper, 9 x 12 or 12 x 18
  (one per student)
- Scrap paper for brainstorming
  ideas

Math Focus

Number and Operations
Understand numbers, ways of
representing numbers, relationships among numbers, and number
systems
- Count with understanding and
  recognize "how many" in sets of
  objects
- Connect number words and
  numerals to the quantities they
  represent, using various physical
  models and representations

Representation
Create and use representations to
organize, record, and communicate
mathematical ideas

Learning Center 1

You will need these materials:

- Pencil
- Crayons
- What I saw worksheet
- *Each Orange Had 8 Slices*
- Drawing paper for our class book
- Scrap paper

1. Look at the story with your friends.
   Talk about the places where the story happened.

2. Think of a place… a house, school, soccer field.

3. Think of a thing…a flower, tooth, soccer ball.

4. Think of how many parts it has.

5. Write your answer with a pencil on your worksheet.

6. Draw a picture to match your words. Use lots of color and details.

7. When your picture is done, check your math work with a friend.

8. File your work and quick check, please.

What I Saw

On my way to the _____
place

I saw _____ _____ .
number   thing

Each _____
thing

had _____ .
number and part

How many _____
parts

were there in all? _____
add all together

Name _____

Learning Center 2
Introduction

Directions

Students will select their favorite page from the story *Each Orange Had 8 Slices* and write about what they see on that page. An illustration to represent their favorite page will help them to use numbers and number words as they complete a prepared page that duplicates the language of the story.

Materials

- *Each Orange Had 8 Slices* (one per student)
- Pencils
- Crayons
- Student worksheet: My favorite page
- Student worksheet: My story

Math Focus

Number and Operations
Understand numbers, ways of representing numbers, relationships among numbers, and number systems
- Count with understanding and recognize "how many" in sets of objects
- Develop understanding of the relative position and magnitude of whole numbers and of ordinal and cardinal numbers and their connections
- Connect number words and numerals to the quantities they represent, using various physical models and representations

Problem Solving
Build new mathematical knowledge through problem solving
- Solve problems that arise in mathematics and in other contexts

Algebra
Use mathematical models to represent and understand quantitative relationships
- Model situations that involve the addition and subtraction of whole numbers, using objects, pictures, and symbols

Learning Center 2

You will need these materials:
- Pencil
- My favorite page
- My story worksheet
- *Each Orange Had 8 Slices*
- Crayons

1. Read the book with your friends at the center.

2. Pick YOUR favorite page and share it with your friends.

3. Write on your favorite page worksheet what you read and see.

4. Answer the questions on your worksheet. Use numbers and number words (**one**, **two**) to write.

5. Draw a picture to match your math sentences.

6. Read your picture and sentences to your friends.

7. File your work and quick check, please.

My Favorite Page

My favorite page in *Each Orange Had 8 Slices* looks like this:

Name _____

My Story

I can write a story to match!

On my way to the _____ ,

I saw _____ and _____ .

Each _____ had _____ .

Each _____ had _____ .

How many _____ were there?

How many _____ were there?

How many _____ were there in all?

Name _____

Learning Center 3
Introduction

Directions

In *Each Orange Had 8 Slices* there are many descriptive words that add color and detail to each page. The students will focus on those descriptive words as they complete a table that encourages recognition and use of adjectives and reinforces number and number word recognition.

Materials

- Student worksheet: Adjective adventure (one per student)
- Pencils
- Crayons
- *Each Orange Had 8 Slices* (one per student)

Math Focus

Data Analysis and Probability
Formulate questions that can be addressed with data and collect, organize, and display relevant data to answer them
- Represent data using concrete objects, pictures, and graphs

Number and Operations
Understand numbers, ways of representing numbers, relationships among numbers, and number systems
- Count with understanding and recognize "how many" in sets of objects

Problem Solving
Apply and adapt a variety of appropriate strategies to solve problems

Learning Center 3

You will need these materials:

- Pencil
- Crayons
- Adjective Adventure
- *Each Orange Had 8 Slices*

1. Look carefully at each page as you read the book with your friends.

2. You are ready to go on an **Adjective Adventure**!

3. Find the words in the book that describe or help you to see the words.

4. Using your pencil, write the describing word from the book on your paper in the correct square.

5. Does the word you wrote make sense?

6. Draw a picture with crayons to match the describing word and the word on your paper.

7. **You are an *Adjective Adventurer!***

8. File your work and quick check, please.

_____ 's

your name

Adjective Adventure!

Draw your own
pictures here ↓

s _____	legs	
r _____	flowers	
l _____	kids	
f _____	cows	
c _____	clowns	
y _____	houses	
j _____	oranges	
s _____	eggs	

Learning Center 4
Introduction

Directions

Using the book *Each Orange Had 8 Slices* the students will complete an alpha chart. The students will look through the book and find words that begin with each letter of the alphabet and fill in their chart. High-frequency words may easily be included, but the challenge of identifying new and unique words that the student may be unfamiliar with will certainly enrich writing vocabulary.

Materials

- *Each Orange Had 8 Slices* (one per student)
- *Student worksheet:* Alpha-chart (one per student; enlarge to 11 x 17 if possible)
- Pencils

Math Focus

Data Analysis and Probability
Formulate questions that can be addressed with data and collect, organize, and display relevant data to answer them
- Sort and classify objects according to their attributes and organize data about the objects

Select and use appropriate statistical methods to analyze data
- Describe parts of the data and the set of data as a whole to determine what the data show

Number and Operations
Understand numbers, ways of representing numbers, relationships among numbers, and number systems
- Count with understanding and recognize "how many" in sets of objects

Learning Center 4

You will need these materials:
- Pencil
- Alpha chart
- *Each Orange Had 8 Slices*

1. Read the book with your friends.

2. Find words in the book that begin with each letter of the alphabet. Fill in your alpha chart. Use a pencil to print the word in the correct box.

3. Do you have any boxes that are empty? Take a second look!

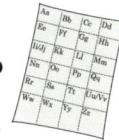

4. Read your alpha chart to your friends.

5. File your work and quick check, please.

Alpha Chart

Aa	Bb
Cc	Dd
Ee	Ff
Gg	Hh
Ii	Jj
Kk	Ll
Mm	Nn

Name _____

Alpha Chart

Oo	Pp
Qq	Rr
Ss	Tt
Uu	Vv
Ww	Xx
Yy	Zz

Name _____

Learning Center 5
Introduction

Directions

Using a familiar object from the story, the orange, the students will demonstrate their understanding of basic division and equal parts as they visually divide the orange into segments. They will write the number and number word next to their drawing of the orange.

Materials

- Student worksheet: Orange segments (one per student)
- Pencils
- Crayons
- Straight-edged object (ruler, stick, narrow oak tag strip)

Math Focus

Number and Operations

Understand numbers, ways of representing numbers, relationships among numbers, and number systems
- Understand and represent commonly used fractions such as $\frac{1}{4}$, $\frac{1}{3}$, and $\frac{1}{2}$

Understand meanings of operations and how they relate to one another
- Understand situations that entail multiplication and division, such as equal groupings of objects and sharing equally

Learning Center 5

You will need the following materials:
- Straight-edged stick or ruler | 1 2 3 4 5 6 7 8 9 10 11 12 |
- Orange segments worksheet *Worksheet*
- Crayon CRAYON
- Pencil

1. You will divide an orange into equal (=) parts.
    The first orange is done for you. It looks like this:

    Use a pencil to write the number of parts (**2**), and
    the number word (**two**).

    Draw another orange. Divide it into
    four equal (=) parts. Continue drawing and dividing
    your oranges until you reach 12 parts. | 1 2 3 4 5 6 7 8 9 10 11 12 |

3. Check your pictures and ideas about division with
    a friend. Read your ideas and your words to
    each other.

4. File your work and quick check, please. *Quick Check* ✔

Orange Segments

I can divide an orange into two (2) equal slices.

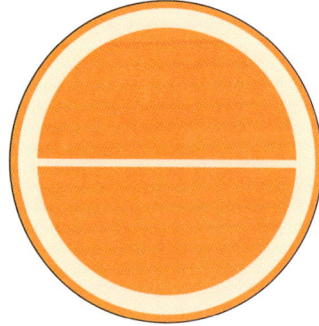

two
2

I can divide an orange into four (4) equal slices.

I can divide an orange into six (6) equal slices.

Name _____

Orange Segments

I can divide an orange into eight (8) equal slices.

I can divide an orange into ten (10) equal slices.

I can divide an orange into twelve (12) equal slices.

Name _____

Learning Center 6
Introduction

Directions

This activity focuses on students as proofreaders. Having been introduced to proofreading symbols through a variety of writing activities, the students will become editors. The editor's work page has many mistakes that are just waiting to be found. Writing the sentences correctly by using the book *Each Orange Had 8 Slices* will be quite a challenge.

Materials

- *Each Orange Had 8 Slices* (one per student)
- Resource page: Proofreading symbols (one per student)
- Student worksheet: Editor's page (one per student)
- Colored pencil
- Pencil

Math Focus

Number and Operations
Understand numbers, ways of representing numbers, relationships among numbers, and number systems
- Count with understanding and recognize "how many" in sets of objects

Learning Center 6

You will need these materials:

- Pencil
- Colored pencil
- Editor's page
- *Each Orange Had 8 Slices*
- Proofreading sheet

1. You are an editor. On your editor's page there are many mistakes. Can you find them?

2. Look at the first sentence. It looks like this:

   "on my way to the pay ground i saw 3 read flowers"

3. Use your proofreading sheet and your colored pencil to help you find and fix the mistakes.

4. Write the sentence the correct way below your edited sentence.

5. Check your work by using your copy of *Each Orange Had 8 Slices*.

6. File your work and quick check, please.

Proofreading Symbols

Take it out

I'm a ~~good~~ good student.

Put something in

good

I'm a ∧ student.

Put in a space

I'm agood student.

Add a period

I'm a good student⊙

Make this letter a capital

i'm a good student.
=

Make this letter lower case

I'm a Good student.

Editor's Page

1. on my way to the pay ground i saw 3 read flowers

2. each duck had 4 babby ducks trailing behind?

3. how many color ful clown were there!

4. on my way to lunch I eight 2 juicy orange

5. how many trees were there.

6. EACH page had 1 prette picture

Name _____

Quick Checks for

Each Orange Had 8 Slices

Learning Center 1 _____

Learning Center 2 _____

Learning Center 3 _____

Learning Center 4 _____

Learning Center 5 _____

Learning Center 6 _____

Name _____

Learning Center 1 Quick Check

1. I brainstormed my ideas before
   I wrote my class book page.   **YES**   **NO**

2. I used colorful details in my picture. **YES**   **NO**

3. My idea is different from the
   other friends' ideas at my table.   **YES**   **NO**

4. My place was a _____ .

5. My thing was a _____ .

6. I checked my math work.   **YES**   **NO**

Name _____

Quick Check ✓

1. Is your picture at the beginning, middle, or end of the story? Write your answer in a sentence:

_____

_____

_____

2. The smallest number on my page is _____ .

3. The greatest number on my page is _____ .

Name _____

Quick
Check

1. There are eight (8) rows on the Adjective Adventure page. Each row has three (3) squares.

   How many squares are there in all? _____

2. What is your favorite adjective from the adjective adventure?

   _____

3. Write a sentence using your favorite word:

   _____

   _____

   _____

Name _____

Quick
Check

1. Which squares on your alpha chart have no words in them? Write the letters of those squares:

    _____

2. Which squares on your alpha chart have more than five (5) words? Write the letters of those squares:

    _____

Name _____

Quick
Check

1.   Write the title of this book.

_____

2.   Draw a picture to match the title of the book.

Name _____

1. How many of your sentences
    ended with a period (.) ? _____

2. How many of your sentences
    ended with a question mark (?) ? _____

3. How many sentences did you correct in all? _____

Congratulations! You are an editor!

Name _____

The Grouchy Ladybug

by Eric Carle

• •

As a book for introducing the concept of telling time, *The Grouchy Ladybug* is unparalleled. Because the grouchy ladybug is unwilling to share the aphids with a friendly ladybug, he flies off to find another meal. Each hour of the day as he flies around, he encounters all kinds of animals to fight, but none of them are big enough (or so he says). At the end of the day he finds himself back where he started, hungry and tired, and very happy to share the aphids with the friendly ladybug.

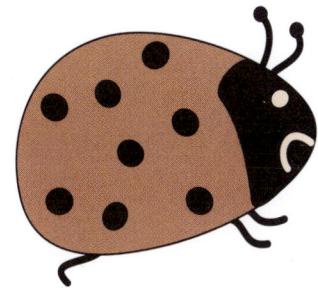

Learning Center 1
Introduction

Directions

The grouchy ladybug meets a variety of animals on his journey to find something to eat. Students will classify the animals that the ladybug met into three categories: land animals, air animals, and water animals. The students will cut and glue the animals on a graph where they label and count the animals.

Materials

- *The Grouchy Ladybug* (one per student)
- Student worksheet: Graph (one per student)
- Resource page: Animals (one per student)
- Scissors
- Glue
- Pencils

Math Focus

Number and Operations
Understand numbers, ways of representing numbers, relationships among numbers, and number systems
- Count with understanding and recognize "how many" in sets of objects
- Develop a sense of whole numbers and represent and use them in flexible ways, including relating, composing, and decomposing numbers

Algebra
Understand patterns, relations, and functions
- Sort, classify, and order objects by size, number, and other properties

Data Analysis and Probability
Formulate questions that can be addressed with data and collect, organize, and display relevant data to answer them
- Sort and classify objects according to their attributes and organize data about the objects
- Represent data using concrete objects, pictures, and graphs

Learning Center 1

You will need these materials:
- Pencils
- Scissors
- Animal page
- *The Grouchy Ladybug*
- Graph
- Glue

1. Using your scissors, cut out the animals along the lines.

2. Glue animals that live on land under **land animals on** the graph.

3. Glue animals that live in the air under **air animals**.

4. Glue animals that live in the water under **water animals**.

5. Label each animal. Their names are in the book.

6. You have made a math graph. Count and write the number of each kind of animal on the bottom of the graph.

7. File your work and quick check, please.

Graph

Land Animals	Air Animals	Water Animals

_____ _____ _____

Name _____

Animal Page

Learning Center 2
Introduction

Directions

The grouchy ladybug starts his journey at 6:00 in the morning and ends his journey right back where he started at 6:00 at night. Every animal the ladybug encounters is met on the hour. This is a great book for the introduction of time. Students will draw the correct time on each of four clocks. They will then draw a picture under each clock representing what they would be doing on a school day during that time. Students will finish the sentence to match their picture.

Materials

- Student worksheet: Clocks (one per student)
- Pencils
- Crayons
- Paper

Math Focus

Measurement

Understand measurable attributes of objects and the units, systems, and processes of measurement
- Recognize the attributes of length, volume, weight, area, and time
- Understand how to measure using nonstandard and standard units

Representation

Create and use representations to organize, record, and communicate mathematical ideas

Learning Center 2

You will need these materials:
- Pencils
- Crayons   CRAYON
- Paper
- Clock page   *Worksheet*

1. Look at the time under the clock on your worksheet. *Worksheet*

2. Draw the clock hands to match the number time.

3. Draw a picture to show what you would be doing at that time of day.

4. Finish this sentence to match your picture:

   I am _____.

5. File your work and quick check, please.   *Quick Check* ✓

Clocks

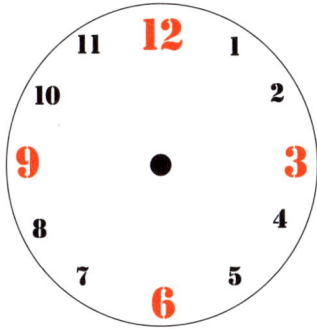

8:00 a.m.

I am _____

_____

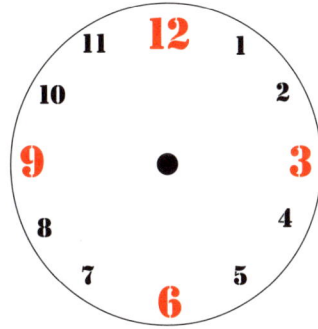

11:00 a.m.

I am _____

_____

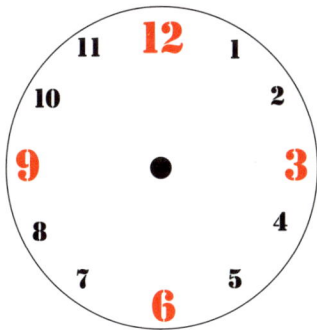

4:00 p.m.

I am _____

_____

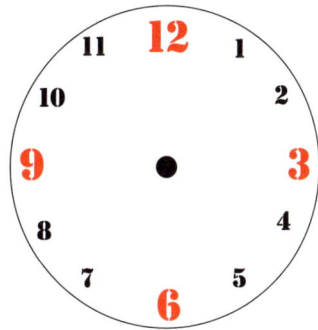

7:00 p.m.

I am _____

_____

Name _____

Learning Center 3
Introduction

Directions

In this activity, your students will pick a time when they are especially grouchy. Maybe that time is when they get up in the morning... or when they go outdoors for recess in cold weather... or when they have to wait for supper... or when they have to go to bed.

Students will draw clocks and grouchy ladybug faces on the clocks. They will then write the numbers 1–12 around their clocks and attach the long and short hands. The students will set their clocks for a time of the day when they are grouchy and write a sentence on their sentence strip telling why they are grouchy then.

Materials

- Student worksheet: Clock (one per student, copied on card stock)
- Crayons
- Scissors
- Brads (one per student)
- Pencils
- Sentence strips
- Clock model (optional)

Math Focus

Measurement
Understand measurable attributes of objects and the units, systems, and processes of measurement
- Recognize the attributes of length, volume, weight, area, and time
- Understand how to measure using nonstandard and standard units

Learning Center 3

You will need these materials:

- Pencils
- Crayons
- Scissors
- Brads
- Sentence strip
- Clock

1. Write the numbers from 1–12 on your clock using your pencil. Some numbers have been written for you.

2. Draw a grouchy ladybug face on your clock using your crayons.

3. Using your scissors, cut out your clock and clock hands.

4. Put one brad through the small hand, the large hand, and the center of your clock.

5. Set the clock for a time of the day when you are grouchy.

6. Write a sentence on your sentence strip telling why you are grouchy at that time.

7. File your work and quick check, please.

Clock

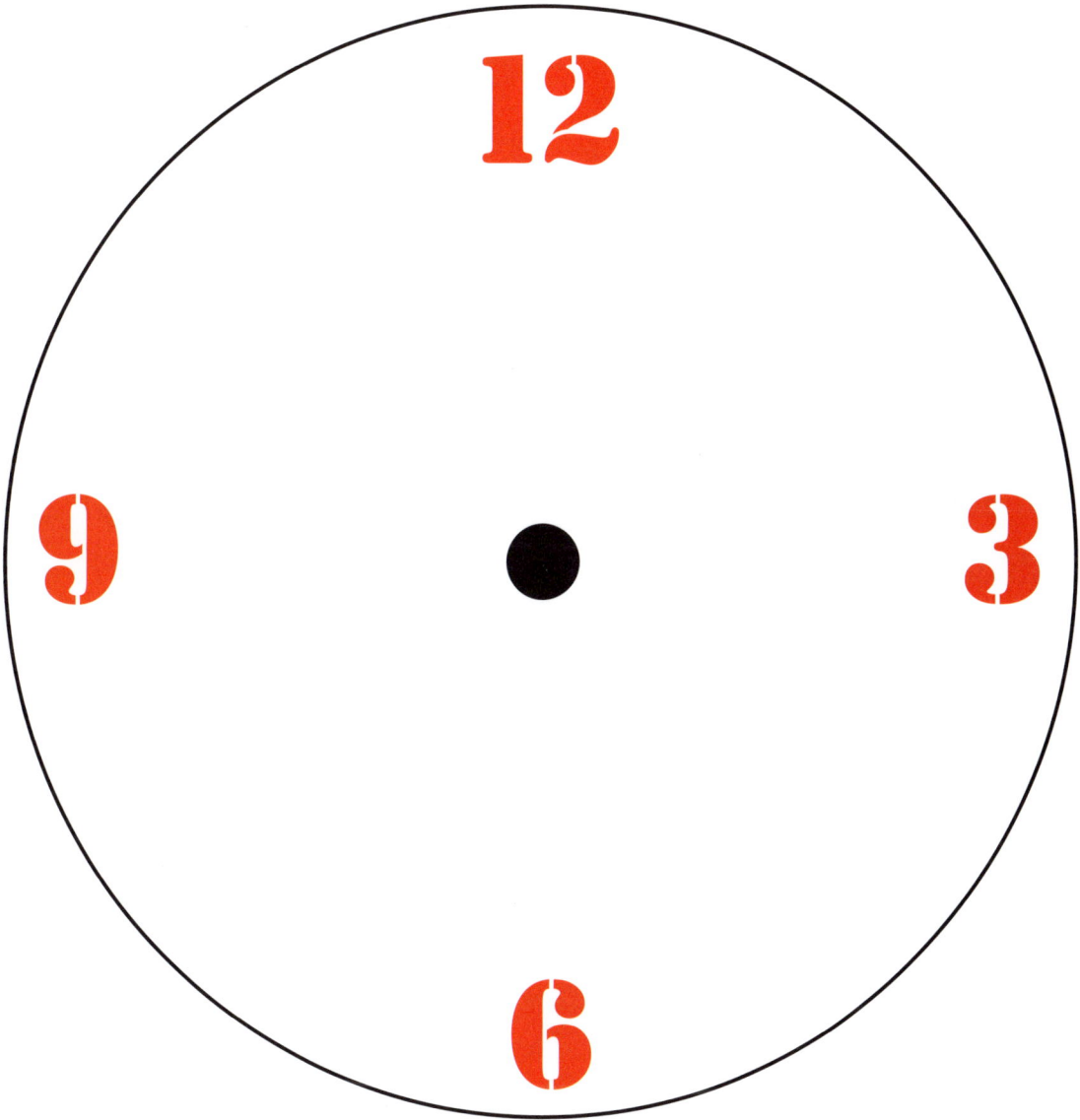

Learning Center 4
Introduction

Directions

The Grouchy Ladybug features a wide variety of animals from insects, birds, and reptiles to crustaceans and mammals. This is a great opportunity for introducing beginning writers to the world of research. Students will choose an animal from the animal books in this center. Using picture clues, the students will answer questions about their animal, ending with a sentence stating a fact about their animal.

Materials
- *The Grouchy Ladybug* (one per student)
- Animal books
- Pencils
- Student worksheet: My animal (one per student)

Math Focus

Number and Operations
Understand numbers, ways of representing numbers, relationships among numbers, and number systems
- Count with understanding and recognize "how many" in sets of objects

Learning Center 4

You will need these materials:
- Pencil
- *The Grouchy Ladybug*
- Animal books
- Animal worksheet

1. Look at the animal books.

2. Choose an animal.

3. Answer the questions on your worksheet. The books will help you with the answers.

4. File your work and quick check, please.

My Animal

My animal is a _____ .

My animal has _____ legs.

My animal has _____ eyes .

My animal has fur.   **Yes**   **No**

My animal has wings.   **Yes**   **No**

My animal eats meat.   **Yes**   **No**

My animal eats plants.   **Yes**   **No**

My animal lays eggs.   **Yes**   **No**

Write one fact about your animal. _____

_____

_____

Name _____

Learning Center 5
Introduction

Directions

By adding one describing word to each sentence, students are introduced to descriptive writing and are able to see how a growing algebraic pattern is generated. Students cut out each sentence and paste the sentences in order by the number of words. The finished paper should appear as follows:

- I saw a ladybug.
- I saw a grouchy ladybug.
- I saw a grouchy ladybug eating.
- I saw a grouchy ladybug eating aphids.
- I saw a grouchy ladybug eating yummy aphids.
- I saw a grouchy ladybug eating nine yummy aphids.

Materials

- Student worksheet: What I saw (one per student)
- Drawing paper, large (one per student)
- Scissors
- Glue

Math Focus

Number and Operations
Understand numbers, ways of representing numbers, relationships among numbers, and number systems
- Count with understanding and recognize "how many" in sets of objects

Algebra
Understand patterns, relations, and functions
- Recognize, describe, and extend patterns such as sequences of sounds and shapes or simple numeric patterns; translate from one representation to another
- Analyze how both repeating and growing patterns are generated

Learning Center 5

You will need these materials:
- Scissors
- Glue
- What I saw worksheet
- Drawing paper

1. Cut your worksheet on the dotted - - - - - - - lines.

2. Find the sentence that has four (4) words. Glue the sentence on the top of your big paper.

3. Find the sentence that has 5 (five) words, and glue it on your big paper under the first sentence.

4. Find the sentences that have six (6), seven (7), eight (8), and nine (9) words. Glue the sentences in order from shortest to longest.

5. When you are done, read your sentences to a friend.

6. File your work and quick check, please.

What I Saw

I saw a ladybug.

I saw a grouchy ladybug eating aphids.

I saw a grouchy ladybug.

I saw a grouchy ladybug eating nine (9) delicious aphids.

I saw a grouchy ladybug eating.

I saw a grouchy ladybug eating delicious aphids.

Name _____

Learning Center 6
Introduction

Directions

The ladybug always repeated the same words to each animal he met. The animals always made the same reply. As you read the story, your students will enjoy repeating the words of predictable print.

In the learning center, students cut and paste the sentences in the same order they were said by the ladybug and other animals. At the end of each sentence, students count and record the number of words.

Materials

- *The Grouchy Ladybug* (one per student)
- Student worksheet: Story
- Drawing paper
- Scissors
- Glue
- Pencils

Math Focus

Number and Operations
Understand numbers, ways of representing numbers, relationships among numbers, and number systems
- Count with understanding and recognize "how many" in sets of objects

Learning Center 6

You will need these materials:
- Scissors
- Pencil
- Glue
- Story worksheet
- *The Grouchy Ladybug*
- Drawing paper

1. Cut out the sentences from your worksheet along the dotted lines - - - - - - - - .

2. Glue the sentences in the same order they were said in the story.

3. Count and record the number of words in each sentence on the line.

4. Read your sentences to a friend.

5. File your work and quick check, please.

Story

"Oh, you're not big enough." _____

"Want to fight?" _____

"Hey you!" _____

"If you insist." _____

Name _____

The Grouchy Ladybug

Learning Center 1 _____

Learning Center 2 _____

Learning Center 3 _____

Learning Center 4 _____

Learning Center 5 _____

Learning Center 6 _____

Name _____

Quick
Check

1. How many land animals
    did you have on your graph? _____

2. How many air animals
    did you have on your graph? _____

3. How many water animals
    did you have on your graph? _____

4. Which had the **LEAST** number of animals? _____

5. Which had the **MOST** number of animals? _____

Name _____

Quick Check ✓

What time is it???

  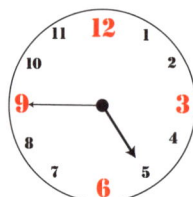 

_____   _____   _____   _____

Name _____

Quick Check ✓

1. On the clock draw the ↱ hands
    to show a time of the day when
    you are happy. ☺

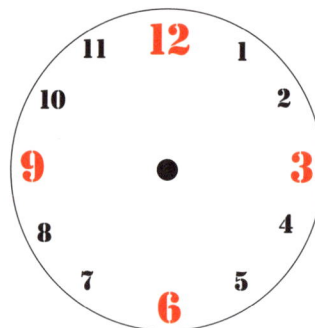

2. Then finish this sentence:
    I am happy when _____

    _____.

Name _____

1. Count all the animals
   the ladybug saw.
   Write the number: _____

2. Count the fireflies at the
   BEGINNING and END of the story.
   Add them together. Write the number: _____

3. How many ladybugs were
   in the story? Write the number: _____

Name _____

Quick
Check
✔

Color ◀ CRAYON the squares to make a pattern:
  red
  red, green
  red, green, blue
  red, green, blue, yellow.

Add a **new** color at the end of each row to build your pattern.

Name _____

Quick Check

What would you say to the ladybug if she asked you to fight? Write your own sentence using quotation marks " ".

_____

_____

_____

_____

_____

Name _____

Bibliography

Carle, E. (1977). *The grouchy ladybug*. New York, NY: Scholastic.

Giganti, P. (Author), & Crews, D. (Illustrator). (1992). *Each orange had 8 slices*. New York, NY: Greenwillow Books.

Hutchins, P. (1986). *The doorbell rang*. New York, NY: Greenwillow Books.

Martin, B., Jr., Sampson, M. (Authors), & Ehlert, L. (Illustrator). (2004). *Chicka chicka 1, 2, 3*. New York, NY: Simon & Schuster Books for Young Readers.

Pinczes, E.J. (Author), & MacKain, B. (Illustrator). (1993). *One hundred hungry ants*. Boston, MA: Houghton Mifflin.

Viorst, J. (Author), & Cruz, R. (Illustrator). (1978). *Alexander who used to be rich last Sunday*. New York, NY: Macmillan.

Rubric

1. Experimenting

I like apples.

Ideas
Uses pictures/scribbles for writing

Organization
Draws/scribbles/scrawls randomly on paper

Voice
Produces unclear work or it is like everyone else's

Word Choice
Uses pictures for words; student can read his/her writing

Sentence Fluency
Mimics letters and words on page

Conventions
Attempts spacing, left to right writing, and top to bottom placement

2. Emerging

I like apples.

Ideas
Represents detailed pictures by some recognizable letters and words

Organization
Begins to group orally and visually like words and pictures

Voice
Displays self-expression through unique pictures and letters

Word Choice
Uses environmental print and some letters to represent words

Sentence Fluency
Strings random letters together to imitate sentence structure

Conventions
Does not use letters to represent sound; beginning use of spacing and placement of words on paper

3. Developing

 I LiKAPL

I like apples.

Ideas
Supports writing with illustration; general idea is understandable

Organization
Represents sequence and events with words and pictures

Voice
Begins to express personal feeling through words and pictures

Word Choice
Repeats familiar words and phrases; uses frequently used words

Sentence Fluency
Uses simple sentence with beginning structure

Conventions
Uses developing phonemic awareness in initial and final consonant placement; random capitalization and punctuation

4. Capable

I like apples.

Ideas
Enhances writing with illustrations; details emerge about topic

Organization
Begins to highlight key ideas, with attempt at beginning and ending and sequencing

Voice
Writes to convey a story with individual/personal expression

Word Choice
Begins to use new, favorite, special descriptive words to create images

Sentence Fluency
Varies beginning and ending of sentences to create rhythm and flow of words

Conventions
Attempts to use writing conventions (spacing, capitalization, punctuation); readable spelling clearly evident and consistent

5. Experienced

Apples

I like apples. I eat apples.
They are yummy.

I like apples.

Ideas
Uses focused topic with supporting details

Organization
Employs easy-to-follow sequence with clear beginning and end

Voice
Shows personality

Word Choice
Uses high-frequency and everyday words independently; writes using fresh, original words

Sentence Fluency
Uses correct sentence structure showing clear idea

Conventions
Uses consistent punctuation, capitals, and spacing

More Great 6+1 Trait® Writing Products

Wee Can Count™

Item #E001
Member $22.65 + shipping / **Nonmember** $25.70 + shipping

Wee Can Write™

This best-selling publication has been widely embraced by teachers of beginning writers across the country. Authors Carolyn McMahon and Peggy Warrick—with a combined 33 years in the elementary-level classroom—wrote the book to fill the need for practical, easy-to-use instructional strageties to introduce the 6+1 Trait® Writing assessment model to their youngest writers. The teacher guide is organized around 36 renowned and readily available picture books, thematically categorized by the four seasons of the year. For each book title, activities are provided for the six traits of writing—skills that form the basis of effective writing at all ages and grade levels. Text is color-coded, making it easy to distinguish information for the teacher versus instruction to be delivered to the students. (2005, 130 pp.)
Item #E009
Member $22.65 + shipping / **Nonmember** $25.70 + shipping

Picture Books

The latest edition of this perennial favorite contains an additional 150 annotations of picture books published between 1998 and 2004. The new annotations include many books suitable for use with young adult readers and listeners, indicated with a 'YA' coding. As in the past, the descriptions are arranged by trait. Each of the traits has sample lesson plans for immediate classroom use, including the recently added "Presentation" trait. If you have started using the 6+1 Trait® Writing Model in your classroom, you will find *Picture Books* an invaluable resource.
Item #E013
Member $16.75 + shipping / **Nonmember** $18.45 + shipping

Seeing With New Eyes

For primary students, writing can take many forms: drawings, scribbles, recordings, and text that goes every which way. The challenge for teachers is to see the experimentation and playfulness of young writers not as errors, but as ways of learning. The sixth edition of *Seeing With New Eyes* is designed to do just that. This 6+1 Trait® Writing guidebook helps teachers use the traits of good writing as a framework for instruction and scoring of prewriters as well as competent ones. While the main audience for the publication is K–2 teachers, the model can also be used for older youngsters in special education and Limited English Proficiency classes. Among the changes to the sixth edition are new scoring guides geared to giving effective feedback on a wide range of student work samples. Using the traits helps teachers focus their instruction, identifying the specific characteristics that contribute to good writing. (2005, 6th ed.; 317 pp.)
Item #E028
Member $23.40 + shipping / **Nonmember** $26.45 + shipping

6+1 Trait® Writing: A Model That Works Video Set

Used in hundreds of classrooms throughout the country, the 6+1 Trait® Writing assessment model works with current curriculum so teachers can accurately assess student writing growth, provide specific, meaningful feedback on student writing, and make appropriate decisions on lesson planning and instructional design. This comprehensive video set provides tools and instruction to implement the 6+1 Trait® Writing Model in grades 2 through 12 and beyond. This professional, 8-tape set includes an introduction to the powerful 6+1 Trait® model, 7 trait-specific videotapes, and a Facilitator's Guide. Each 8-minute, trait-specific video:

* Clearly defines one trait
* Summarizes the characteristics of the traits
* Describes how good use of the trait looks
* Explains scoring criteria illustrated with examples of actual student writing
* Provides practice scoring opportunities
* Offers insights from teachers using the model

The Facilitator's Guide reinforces and supplements the video series with scoring guides, samples of scored student writing, and instructions on how to optimize use of the videos. (2003; 144 pp.)
Item #E300
Member $399.60 + $12.99 shipping
Nonmember $424.00 + $12.99 shipping

6+1 Trait® Writing Rubric to Grade Converter

Teachers love a lot of things about the 6+1 Trait® model: It helps them improve their writing instruction; it shows students what good writing looks like; and it creates a common vocabulary to discuss writing. But, the main drawback to the model has always been the time-consuming calculations required to convert rubric scores to grades. NWREL offers a time-saving solution that ensures accuracy using reliable slide-chart technology. The Rubric to Grade Converter has the flexibility to work with the model's four-, five-, and six-point scales and can be used to grade writing on just one or up to all seven traits. (2005; 4 by 9 inches)
Item #E112
Member $9.75 + shipping / **Nonmember** $10.60 + shipping

NWREL Product Order Form

1 HOW WILL YOU ORDER?

Fax this form (for credit card and purchase orders) to: (503) 275-0458
Or, mail this form (for credit card, purchase order, check, or cash orders) to:
Northwest Regional Educational Laboratory Marketing Office, 101 S.W. Main Street, Ste. 500, Portland, OR 97204-3297
ALL SALES ARE FINAL AND RETURNS CANNOT BE ACCEPTED. REVIEW COPIES CANNOT BE PROVIDED.

2 HOW CAN WE CONTACT YOU?

Shipping Address: (please print or type)   **Billing Address**: (if different than shipping address)

Name _____

Institution _____

Street address _____

City, state, ZIP _____

Daytime phone number _____   E-mail address _____

3 WHAT ITEMS ARE YOU ORDERING?

Item #	Title	Quantity	Price	Subtotal

To receive the member discount, items must be shipped to an address in Oregon, Washington, Montana, Idaho, or Alaska.

Subtotal ordered $ _____

Postage and shipping (see above) $ _____

Total $ _____

4 HOW MUCH IS POSTAGE AND SHIPPING?

- Orders are processed and shipped within 7 days.
- Rush orders (shipped within 24 hours) have additional 25% processing fee plus added shipping cost.
- Orders shipped to locations in the United States where UPS delivery is not available will be shipped via first-class U.S. mail at the UPS ground rate.
- Orders shipped outside the United States, its possessions, and Canada are shipped via international air mail and require an additional 25% shipping charge.

Merchandise Subtotal	UPS Ground (10–14 days)	Third-Day UPS Air	Second-Day UPS Air
Less than $14.99	$ 4.50	$ 9.95	$17.45
$15.00–24.99	$ 6.50	$10.95	$18.45
$25.00–39.99	$ 8.50	$13.95	$21.45
$40.00–69.99	$11.50	$16.95	$24.45
$70.00–99.99	$15.50	$20.95	$28.45
$100.00–199.99	$19.50	$24.95	$32.45
$200.00 or more	10% of total	15% of total	20% of total

5 HOW ARE YOU PAYING?

❑ Purchase order from U.S. institution   ❑ Prepayment in U.S. dollars/check enclosed   ❑ VISA/MasterCard credit card (circle one)

PO # _____   (copy of purchase order must be enclosed)

Credit card number _____   Expiration date _____

Printed name on card _____   Signature _____

Daytime phone number _____   Member institution _____

Wee Can Write Workshops

Full-Day Workshop

In this full-day workshop, the 6+1 Trait® Writing Model and teaching ideas will be presented using familiar literature titles that your youngest students love. You will practice using the traits through oral language, reading, listening, and writing activities that will leave you comfortable using the writing traits, and increase the ability of your students to communicate. The vocabulary of 6+1 Trait® Writing will be an added focus. These are the common words that are used to talk to your students about writing each day, and will provide them with a solid foundation for writing throughout their school lives. You will learn a wealth of activities using award-winning literature titles found in your library or on your personal bookshelf that are flexible, creative, and take no more than three to five minutes to prepare. Learn about the traits today…use them tomorrow!

Two-Day Workshop

In this two-day training, the workshop facilitator will demonstrate a variety of listening, speaking, reading, and writing activities that will strengthen and enhance your young students' beginning writing. You will leave feeling confident and comfortable using the writing traits as you increase the ability of your students to communicate. Additionally, an introduction to the trait language—common words to use when talking to your students about writing—will provide you with a solid foundation for writing with your students across the curriculum, throughout the school day, and through their school lives.

Work and share with other teachers as you experiment with a range of practical, low-preparation, and creative writing activities. This is a "learn it today…use it tomorrow" workshop! You will discover how adaptable these activities are—modify them to use with other familiar and favorite children's literature titles already on your classroom bookshelf!

For more information about Using Wee Can Write™ and other 6+1 Trait® workshops, contact Doris Mellor at 503-275-9187 or mellord@nwrel.org

Wee Can Write™ Classroom Poster

Teachers using *Wee Can Write™* can jazz up their classrooms while reinforcing the traits of good writing with the new *Wee Can Write™* Classroom Poster. This cheerful 18 x 24-inch poster highlights each of the six traits and delivers a blast of student-friendly guidance about writing with the traits.

Code: E005

Member:
$8.50 plus
shipping

Nonmember:
$9.50 plus
shipping

Wee Can Write™

Ideas
My writing and pictures have lots of details. *Do my words match the pictures?*

Word Choice
My words help me hear the story! *Did I choose the words that paint a picture for my reader?*

Organization
My story has a beginning, a middle, and an ending. *Does my paper look neat?*

Sentence Fluency
My sentences go together and make sense. *Do my sentences flow and grow and follow the story?*

Voice
My writing sounds like me! WOW! *Did I write with my own words and expression?*

Conventions
My sentences go from left to right. *Did I use capital letters, spaces between words, and the correct punctuation?*

NWREL
Northwest Regional Educational Laboratory
101 S.W. Main Street
Suite 500
Portland, Oregon 97204
503-275-9500
info@nwrel.org
www.thetraits.org

The information on this poster is from *Wee Can Write* written by Carolyn McMahon and Peggy Warrick.

Wee Can Write™ Continuum Posters

This set of five posters shows "wee writers" what good writing looks like along the Wee Writers' Continuum featured in *Wee Can Write*™ from "experimenting" to "experienced." Each 18 x 24-inch poster shows what each trait looks like along the continuum to teach students how to move their writing to the next level.

Code: E006

Member: $17.50 plus shipping

Nonmember: $19.00 plus shipping

Wee Can Write™ Poster Pack

Get a special price on the *Wee Can Write*™ Classroom Poster and the Wee Writers' Continuum when you purchase together.

Code: E007

Member: $21.50 plus shipping

Nonmember: $24.00 plus shipping

Wee Can Count™ Student Instruction Set

Each of the 36 student activity instruction sheets from *Wee Can Count*™ is beautifully presented in color and laminated for durability. Instead of photocopying the student activities from the book in either dull black and white or expensive color, use these sheets. They're cheerful and ready for action, and can be used over and over for years! (2007; 36 pp.)

Item #E003

Member

$28.00 plus shipping

Nonmember

$31.00 plus shipping

Activity 1

You will need these materials:
- Pencils
- Crayons
- *One Hundred Hungry Ants*
- Paper

1. Read and retell *One Hundred Hungry Ants* with your friends.

2. Draw a detailed picture to tell about what you see in *One Hundred Hungry Ants*. Use crayons and paper.

3. Draw your favorite animals from the story.

4. Add three (3) trees.

5. Add six (6) ants.

6. Add one (1) picnic basket.

7. Write a YUMMY sentence to describe your picture.

8. File your work and quick check, please.